ONE BELT ONE ROAD
China's Long March Toward 2049

Michael H. Glantz
University of Colorado, Boulder
Consortium for Capacity Building (CCB)

with
Robert J. Ross
and
Gavin G. Daugherty

A Greenbank Book
2019

ONE BELT ONE ROAD
China's Long March Toward 2049
Michael H. Glantz
with Robert J. Ross and Gavin G. Daugherty

ISBN: 978-1-896559-47-6

Editing & design: John Negru
Cover photo: Lisa Benson Editorial Cartoon used with the permission of Lisa Benson,
the Washington Post Writers Group and the Cartoonist Group. All rights reserved.

A Greenbank Book

Published by
The Sumeru Press Inc.
402-301 Bayrose Drive, Nepean, ON
Canada K2J 5W3

LIBRARY AND ARCHIVES CANADA CATALOGUING IN PUBLICATION

Title: One Belt One Road : China's long march toward 2049 / Michael H. Glantz (University of
Colorado, Boulder), with Gavin G. Daugherty and Robert J. Ross.
Names: Glantz, Michael H., author. | Daugherty, Gavin G., author. | Ross, Robert J., 1990- author.
Description: A Greenbank Book. | Includes bibliographical references.
Identifiers: Canadiana 20190088885 | ISBN 9781896559476 (softcover)
Subjects: LCSH: Yi dai yi lu (Initiative : China) | LCSH: China—Foreign economic relations—Eurasia.
| LCSH: Eurasia—Foreign economic relations—China.
Classification: LCC HF1604 .G63 2019 | DDC 337.51—dc23

For more information about The Sumeru Press
visit us at *sumeru-books.com*

Contents

PART I
Origins of the One Belt One Road Initiative

PART II
Concepts of OBOR/BRI

PART III
The Great Games

PART IV
Concluding Comments

APPENDICES

Preface

The notion of OBOR (One Belt One Road) was launched as an initiative in 2013 by the newly elected General Secretary of the Chinese Communist Party and President, Xi Jinping. It captured my attention in mid-2015. The more I learned about it, the more intrigued I became. International interest in OBOR grew sharply, as witnessed by the increasing news coverage worldwide, as well as the number of countries that want to participate. China's bilateral loan arrangements for the construction of sorely-needed transportation infrastructure projects were very appealing to the leaders of developing economies.

The idea behind the One Belt One Road, initially at least, was to increase China's trade with European countries. The symbol of the ancient silk road was invoked to energize Chinese citizens, companies, banks and provinces by highlighting a bright spot in China's long history. In retrospect, it evolved into a plan for China to become a global superpower.

OBOR connectivity through the funding of infrastructure projects would involve Asian, Middle Eastern, and Northeastern African countries. The more I continued to read about OBOR, the more confusing it became to capture the full socio-economic and political aspects of OBOR, which was later relabeled as the Belt and Road Initiative (BRI). To understand the various geographic and functional dimensions of OBOR/BRI, we refer to China's worldwide infrastructure development programs as "Great Games," a reference to the 19th century political and military competition in Central Asia between the Russian and the British empires.

This primer introduces the reader to various aspects of the Belt and Road Initiative, including references that enable readers to pursue specific aspects of interest. It relies on popular news articles and reports and allows various writers and political cartoonists to speak in their own words and images, respectively.

After five years of OBOR/BRI projects, questions about success stories and concerns about failure began to appear more frequently. Requests to renegotiate original agreements are increasing, as well as demands for increased scrutiny of infrastructure-related development loan offers. The most stinging accusation to date appears to be one involving the notion of "debt traps," that is, a situation in which the borrowers cannot pay the installments on the loan and must give up its ownership of the property for which the loan had been taken. The lender, in this case China, takes over the operation and infrastructure(s) as well as the adjacent trade free zone it had constructed. A seemingly high-risk loan turns into a win for China, suggesting that the hidden agenda was actually a geopolitical win as opposed to an economic win. President Xi continues to claims China's loans are win-win situations, while India, Australia and the US, as well as a small but growing number of OBOR/BRI-funded recipients, continue to warn countries about China's debt traps and debt-trap diplomacy.

For this primer, we do not take sides, when citing various, often competing, articles as reported in the printed, electronic and online media. Our overriding objective is to create public awareness of China's important ongoing global infrastructure development experiment that has its supporters as well as detractors.

Michael H. Glantz
University of Colorado, Boulder
April 2019

Acknowledgements

We appreciate the interest and support of Dr. Igor Zonn, Director of the Water Problems Institute in Moscow, Russia, for translating and publishing my 2017 OBOR paper "One Belt One Road: What a Difference a Brand Makes." We also appreciate Professor Kairat Moldashev (Narxoz University, Kazakhstan) for his written contribution to this primer and Professor Tsegay Wolde-Giorgis (CCB Research Associate) for his contribution to the Africa Great Game section. Zhanara Temirbekova (President of Kazakhstan's Eurasian Technological University) provided insights on Central Asia.

Special appreciation is extended to Prof. Qian Ye, Executive Director of Integrated Risk Governance (IRG) and Beijing Normal University Professor, and to Dr. Tim Sim of Hong Kong Politechnic University (HKPU) whose activities stimulated and fostered our early interest in China's OBOR/BRI project.

A sincere "Thank You" is also for the organizations and political cartoonists who allowed us to use their images, with special appreciation to Craig Stephens and the *South China Morning Post* (Hong Kong) for their contributions to our publication.

Our primer could not have been written without the valuable assistance we received from several individuals and organizations whose contributions were useful and timely: research assistants Alan Linenberger (CSU) and Alexandra Harden (Columbia University) and early discussions about the Greek port of Piraeus with Spiros Tsakos (George Washington University).

This publication could not have been completed without the endless understanding and support of our families for our effort to provide a reader-friendly overview of Chinese President Xi Jinping's "One Road and One Belt Initiative."

My brother Ronnie was a constant supporter and adviser for all my career and research efforts, including for OBOR/BRI. I miss our daily chats on my ride to work.

From OBOR to BRI

This year, 2019, marks the sixth year since the launching of the New Economic Silk Road, President Xi's plan to rejuvenate the image, spirit, success and (more importantly) symbolic value attributed to China's ancient Silk Road. In 2013, China's then-newly-elected President Xi announced his OBOR Initiative in a speech in Astana, Kazakhstan. A month later Xi introduced China's Maritime Silk Road in an address to the Indonesian Parliament. At that time, his stated objective was to rejuvenate the notion of the ancient trade routes between China and Western Europe.

The "Belt" of OBOR represents the ancient trade routes that traversed western China across the Eurasian landmass to Europe and places in-between. The "Road" of OBOR, counterintuitively, is actually a maritime string of ports (sometimes referred to as a "string of pearls") from eastern China, through Southeast, Southwest, and South Asia, the Middle East to Southeastern, Eastern and Western Europe with a branch extending to Kenya and Ethiopia. Once the OBOR Initiative was announced, the number of countries interested in participating grew rapidly. China's successful approach to development through infrastructure modernization had rekindled their hopes for development. The possibility of substantial amounts of China-backed funding meant that their hoped-for development opportunities were becoming a distinct possibility. Meanwhile, China had announced it was ready to commit as much $4 trillion USD for OBOR projects over time.

Fig. 1 President Xi announces his new Silk Road (One Belt One Road) Initiative in 2013. *Consortium for Capacity Building (CCB).*

Fig. 2 Street Artist's Painting of a Silk Road caravan. Turpan, Xinjiang.

From the day OBOR was first announced, it elicited favorable comments from political leaders of Silk Road countries, all of whom were potential OBOR partners.

Geostrategically, the initiative was launched in Astana, Kazakhstan, a former Soviet Union republic, because it was to be a central hub in Xi's New Economic Silk Road vision.

In short order, the China infrastructure and trade initiative had attracted offers of cooperation with China from various leaders along the proposed routes of the belts and roads.

The original acronym, OBOR, had taken on the characteristics of a popular "brand" for a commercial product, a brand that would help China to market the value of its goods and share its engineering know-how and its infrastructure-related construction products and services internationally. If sustained, the OBOR Initiative could accelerate China's (actually, President Xi's) desired ascendance toward becoming a major political as well as economic global power, while still proclaiming itself as the largest and most successful developing country.

It is important to note with regard to this last point the following new development: "China maintains that it is a developing country, but the U.S. argues it belongs among the advanced nations." (Tsuji *et al.*, 2019) They went on to note, "the U.S. argued Thursday that it no longer makes sense for China [a member that has landed a Rover on the dark side of the moon] to receive special World Trade Organization privileges that were originally designed to assist developing countries." The US has recently made similar claims about Turkey and India.

Given the lack of transparency in governmental decision-making processes in general, and more specifically in China, about how such high-level political decisions are really made, it appears that China's OBOR started out to be a regional, intercontinental (Eurasian) trade and infrastructure development assistance initiative. In retrospect, it apparently, by chance, has become a successful brand for China's efforts to create a Eurasian development model. Xi's symbolic use of the ancient Silk Road was meant to build on and foster China's recent and future efforts to "share and sell" its expertise. It would do so through financing trade, manufacturing and the construction of infrastructure such as high-speed railways, highways, ports, airports, inland hubs, pipelines, and energy-producing facilities. It was able to do so using its sizable accumulated foreign reserves due to favorable trade balances with other countries. In return, China would receive access to economic benefits such as raw materials and to economic and political benefits by providing services such as agreements to manage deep-water ports

Fig. 3 Sharing China's wealth via the Initiative with Europe and Africa. *C. Stephens, South China Morning Post (SCMP).*

worldwide. It is increasingly evident that China would also eventually receive military benefits as a result of its favorable (to China) loan arrangements.

Following its initial launching, several observers, e.g., Lowy Institute (2016), suggested that OBOR was like the "Marshall Plan," America's post-WWII plan to rebuild Europe's devastated infrastructure, commerce and societies. This comparison, however, has been challenged by Chinese as well as US and European sources, given the obvious programmatic differences between President Xi's Initiative and the Marshall Plan. Recently, the comparison was challenged during US Senate Armed Services Committee hearings in late 2017:

> It [OBOR] is probably the biggest development program in the world. It's five times the amount of money that the United States put in under the Marshall Plan.... But the difference is the Marshall Plan was philanthropic in nature and was designed to lift up countries in Europe following World War II and One Belt One Road is designed to lift up China....

"The Marshall Plan was not loans primarily. It was philanthropy. [OBOR] investment, the USD $1.2 trillion that's coming, is mostly in the form of loans." (*PTI*, 2018)

Zhang Xiaoqiang, former Deputy Director of the National Development and Reform Commission, was quoted as saying: "China's promotion of the OBOR Initiative will never involve geopolitical games or the formation of a destabilizing group, which differs from the nature of the Marshall Plan." (*Asia Times*, 2018)

Putting aside the political aspects of foreign aid,

Fig. 4 President Xi's OBOR assists to developing countries in their path to economic development. *D. Simmonds, Economist.*

there is a major difference between how China and the United States and Europe view the concept of foreign aid. To the United States aid is not viewed as a business deal but as a political or societal obligation to assist the country receiving the aid in the form of humanitarian assistance, development funding or grants. Aid is in addition to other types of commercial interactions, such as loans.

China's OBOR/BRI version of aid:

...is typical of the pragmatic, profit- (commercial or otherwise) orientated model that has long characterized Chinese aid...which fits perfectly

with Beijing's understanding of "development co-operation." "Development cooperation" consists less of grants and volunteerism, and more of bank loans and the construction expertise of Chinese companies…. In the language of the Party, it is about mutual, "win-win," growth rather than assistance. (Mardell, 2018)

It is clear that China, Europe and the USA have varying opinions of what humanitarian aid is and how it is to be administered.

REFERENCES

 Asia Times, 2018. "Belt and Road differs from Marshall Plan: senior Chinese official." (January 18).

 Lowy Institute, 2016. "One Belt One Road: China's New Marshall Plan to remake Eurasia." (May 29).

 Mardell, J., 2018. "Foreign Aid with Chinese Characteristics." *The Diplomat* (August 7). PTI, 2018. "OBOR partially aims to marginalize US

 Influence in Pacific: Admiral Harry Harris." *The Economic Times* (March 16).

 Tsuji, T., R. Osokawa and T. Hoyama, 2019. "US takes aim at China's status as a developing nation: WTO proposals would eliminate favorable treatment for world's No. 2 economy" *Nikkei Asian Review* (March 2).

Introduction

This book provides a brief overview of China's "One Belt One Road" Initiative (OBOR), now *officially* re-labeled the BRI (Belt and Road Initiative). Looking back from the vantage point of 2019 to 2013, when OBOR was first announced as China's new international infrastructure and trade initiative, OBOR has proven to be nothing less than an eye-catching program to assist developing countries in need of financing for sorely-needed infrastructure to achieve their economic development goals.

Early on, the *Economist* Intelligence Unit (2016) summarized China's proposed infrastructure projects in the following way: "The Belt-Road initiative represents China's official policy for enhancing global supply chains, primarily through infrastructure projects throughout the developing and parts of the developed world." (p. 1) What at first appeared to be development and trade assistance to European as well as Asian and a few African markets has grown tremendously in geographic scope and has accelerated over time. It has since proven to be a display of China's financial, economic, political and technological ambitions and, more recently, its military might.

OBOR has been touted as one of the most ambitious economic development programs since the Marshall Plan was created in 1947 to rebuild a devastated Europe in the aftermath of World War II. *Port Technology* (2018) recently claimed "The One Belt One Road Initiative (BRI) is the single biggest infrastructure redevelopment project in history, and no other state-sponsored enterprise is currently provoking more discussion, dread or excitement."

The already rapid growth rate of China's OBOR received an unanticipated major boost when Donald Trump was elected US President in November 2016 and took office in mid-January 2017. Trump's campaign rhetoric and ensuing policies exposed his support for American isolationism as reflected in his campaign slogan "America First." Since his inauguration, the US has aggressively, intentionally, and incrementally embarked on abandoning its global leadership position and commitments, which it had held since the end of WWII. China through its OBOR has since taken advantage of the geopolitical vacuum created by America's self-imposed abdication not only from its global leadership status but from long-standing regional alliances and trade agreements as well.

Today, more than 70 countries and organizations are involved in the OBOR/BRI enterprise. Each one of these appears to have its own interesting story to tell related to China's support for its infrastructure projects including but not limited to pipelines, high-speed and other rail lines, communications networks, roads, deep-water and air ports, energy grids and inland transport and cargo hubs. China supplies developing countries with the access to loans, construction materials and workers. OBOR/BRI is sold by China as a win-win(-win) situation in which China and the loan recipient benefit economically (with the third win representing peace).

In this book we focus mainly on the international aspects of the OBOR/BRI. However, it is obvious that one cannot isolate the international from the domestic. A brief listing of some domestic issues in the era of OBOR/BRI is necessary, and links to more comprehensive coverage are warranted. Many articles on OBOR cite the drivers for Xi's intensification of China's "going out" policy, as the use of the country's overcapacity of factories developed during its years of outstanding double-digit economic growth rates. With a relative slowdown of its economy starting about 2008, coping with and adjusting to industrial overcapacity and unemployment issues became prominent Communist Party concerns. Fiegenbaum (2018) pointed out some key domestic issues:

When Xi Jinping and his colleagues toss and turn at night, I suspect their major policy nightmares and preoccupations are entirely homegrown: (1) how to stay in power and overcome dissent; (2) how to create some 12 million new jobs each year; (3) how to maintain sufficient growth to support those employment goals; (4) how to manage the demographic challenges of an aging country through welfare and "entitlement" reforms; and (5) how to mitigate pollution and environmental challenges.

In fact, it seems that there has been an increase since early 2018 in the number of articles raising doubts about the ability of President Xi to retain power, citing examples of growing concern if not discontent with various of Xi's domestic policies. Apparently, the articles suggest an emerging vocal in-country opposition to Xi's authoritarian moves, including, but not limited to, his consolidation of power by modifying the Party's constitution, weakening his potential opposition through anti-corruption campaigns, and the fostering of a cult of personality by removing a president's term limits (e.g., *Associated Press News*, 2018). Martin and Crawford (2018) raised this possibility in their article entitled "Is Xi Jinping's Bold China Power Grab Starting to Backfire?" suggesting that:

Today, China's president looks like he may have overreached. An economic slowdown, a tanking stock market, and an infant-vaccine scandal are all feeding domestic discontent, while abroad, in Western capitals and financial centers, there's a growing wariness of Chinese ambitions. And then there is the escalating trade war with the U.S. China initially refused to believe it would happen, but in the past few weeks it's become the prism through which Xi's perceived failings are best projected.

Other media headlines in 2018 also focused on Xi's domestic problems: "Murmurings of Dissent Upset China's Script for Xi's Power Grab" (*New York Times*, May 8, 2018); "Resistance Mounts against Xi Jinping" (*Lima Charlie News*, August 17); "Signs Show "Core Leader Xi Facing Domestic Reproach" (*China Digital Times*, August); "China's president may be weaker than he appears" (*MarketWatch*, July 2); "Xi Jinping Thought is Facing a Harsh Reality Check" (*Foreign Policy*, August 15); "As China's Woes Mount, Xi Jinping Faces Rare Rebuke at Home" (*New York Times*, July 31); and so forth.

Martin and Crawford went on to note a link between the US-China trade war and the OBOR/BRI:

"The trade war has made China more humble," says Wang Yiwei, a professor of international affairs at Renmin University in Beijing and deputy director of the institution's "Xi Jinping Thought" center. "We should keep a low profile," he says, even suggesting that China should rethink how it implements Xi's flagship "Belt and Road" infrastructure project.

It is too early to tell what the immediate, let alone long-term, impacts that the trade war might have on the future success of OBOR/BRI. Nevertheless, speculation abounds. The set of actual media headlines shown below illustrates the range of possible impacts of the US-China trade war on China's "going out" policy.

Weblines that link US-China Trade War to OBOR

- As trade war erupts, China puts brakes on its global domination dream.
- Trade War May Hurt BRI.
- China's BRI faces slowdown following US trade measures.
- Can "One Belt One Road" save China from Trump's Trade Wars?
- Trump's China Policy Has a Flaw: It Makes China the Winner.
- Trump's trade war against China may have a "perverse reaction."
- How Trump's tariffs and WTO threats fuel China's Belt and Road Initiative.
- China sees Trump's trade war as an opportunity to boost ties with Africa.

Although each region, country or project mentioned in this book merits its own book-length, in-depth attention, here we highlight OBOR's geographic and functional stealth-like expansion around the globe on land, sea and in space. An extensive reference list is provided to enable readers to pursue various OBOR/BRI-related topics of interest.

Various concepts of China's expansion will be explored throughout the book. Following a cautionary comment on the mapping of China's initiative, political and military activities in the South China Sea, and activities directly related to China's "going out" policy would be a good place to start.

REFERENCES

 Associated Press News, 2018. "Xi cult of personality unseen in China since Mao" *APNews* (March 11).

 Durden, T., 2018. "China To Take Over Kenya's Largest Port Over Unpaid Chinese Loan." Zero Hedge (Dec 27).

 The Economist Intelligence Unit, 2016. *"One Belt, One Road": An Economic Roadmap*. London, UK (May).

 Fiegenbaum, E.A., 2018. "A Chinese Puzzle: Why Economic "Reform" in Xi's China Has More Meanings Than Market Liberalization." Carnegie Endowment (February 26).

 Martin, P. and A. Crawford, 2018. "Is Xi Jinping's Bold China Power Grab Starting to Backfire?" *Bloomberg* (August 7).

 Port Technology, 2018. "China's Top Three Belt and Road Initiatives." (July 24).

Mapping OBOR/BRI:
The devil is in the details

A search on the Internet for maps depicting the OBOR/BRI network yields hundreds of such images. At first glance, each image appears to be useful. They seem quite similar, highlighting routes of selected cities along the various silk roads and belts. The various road and belt maps can be sub-categorized by their primary characteristics, such as basic transportation networks, highly detailed regions, country-specific, activity-specific, energy-specific, pipeline-specific, railway and road infrastructure-specific, and so on. However, closer scrutiny reveals how they differ from one another. In many cases, they provide neither accurate nor up-to-date information. As pointed out by Iwanek (2018) who reviewed *Xinhua* maps, even maps produced by official Chinese sources are suspect.

Iwanek discussed his concerns about new silk road maps in his article provocatively sub-titled "Why you should ignore Belt and Road Initiative maps." He was concerned about the ease with which map users might uncritically select on the Internet a map even from a supposedly reliable Chinese state agency (such as *Xinhua*) to enhance an article without realizing that the chosen map did not provide accurate or up-to-date information. He convincingly pointed out flaws in official maps to make his point. His article suggested that such maps should carry with them a "user beware" warning label.

Before coming across Iwanek's article, we had intended to prepare some thoughts on OBOR/BRI maps using the subtitle "the devil is in the details." We wanted to make the point that there are few up-to-date, complete,

or accurate maps that encompass all Chinese activities that could be considered, directly or indirectly, a part of OBOR/BRI.

Each map maker gets to choose the information s/he wishes to present to potential map users, as well as the level of its detail. For example, it is difficult to find an OBOR map that includes the Polar Silk Road. Also, as of now very few global maps include official Chinese BRI projects or other BRI-like infrastructure activities in Latin America. China has been courting Latin countries, providing bilateral infrastructure projects with countries whose leaders for the most part have been at odds with the US policy (e.g., Bolivia, Ecuador, Venezuela, and El Salvador), in addition to others sometimes at odds with the US policy (e.g., Panama, Brazil, Peru, Guatemala, and Argentina).

Fig. 5   The Initiative's original six belts and roads. *B. Krajnik, Slovenia Times.*

At the end of a Ministerial Forum between China and CELAC (Community of Latin American and Caribbean States) in January 2018, Myers and Barrios (2018) reported on some important announcements made by China's Foreign Minister about his government's support for countries in the Western Hemisphere:

> …but the region's formal inclusion in China's Belt and Road Initiative (BRI) was not one of them. Chinese officials welcomed Latin America's participation in the Initiative, generating considerable buzz about the region's newfound place on the Belt and Road. However, Chinese officials stopped short of officially including Latin America and the Caribbean [LAC] on their BRI map…. Chinese officials referred to the region as a "natural extension" of the Maritime Silk Road, while adding that the region is *an "indispensable participant" in the construction of the BRI.*" (italics added)

And so, although LAC remains formally outside of the BRI, much of what China is proposing to do in the region is consistent with BRI's stated goals.

Many of the maps in an internet search still focus on the locations of the original six OBOR roads and belts. Several maps show OBOR/BRI projects at a national or regional level. It is fair to note that map makers have a challenge in keeping up with the addition of new OBOR/BRI projects. OBOR/BRI has been changing so fast that even the latest detailed accurate map would likely become incomplete within a month. There seems to be a constant flow of new letters of intent, MOUs, or bilateral agreements being prepared, changed, or cancelled each month between China and OBOR/BRI partners.

For example, the *Eurasian Times* (2018) reported that "Towards the end of the year 2017, China revealed two major proposals under the Belt and Road Initiative (BRI). The first was an extension of Pakistan's China-Pakistan Economic Corridor (CPEC) to Afghanistan and, second, the linking of Chabahar port in Iran with Gwadar port in Pakistan." Increasingly, there have been changes made or requested by some BRI country partners of China to restructure their loans or to downsize their projects in attempts to avoid defaulting on their loan payments. As an example, loan defaults have already occurred, leading to the takeover of some projects by China, as suggested in the following news headline: "China to take over Kenya's largest port over unpaid Chinese loan." (Durden, 2018)

Iwanek (2018) concluded his critique of maps with the following thought: "The Belt and Road Initiative is so complex, differently interpreted and dynamic – incorporating new projects all the time – that we should look for new innovative ways to represent it geographically." Until that happens, users of such maps must be made aware of the sources and the potential biases as well as subliminal messages embedded in those maps.

One notable exception about maintaining comprehensive up-to-date mapping is the Mercator Institute for China Studies (MERICS):

> The MERICS Belt and Road Tracker draws upon a large database of projects within the framework of China's Belt and Road Initiative (BRI). The database contains more than 1000 entities, it is continuously updated and expanded. Updates are based on a systematic monitoring and data collection from a wide set of Chinese and international official sources, industry associations, companies and media…. The MERICS BRI database aims to cover all projects that further BRI goals – regardless of how they are marketed. (www.MERICS.org)

REFERENCES

 Eurasian Times, 2018. "China and India Battle for Global Influence with OBOR and NSTC Projects." (January 18).

 Iwanek, K., 2018. "The New Silk Road Is Old: Why You Should Ignore Belt and Road Initiative Maps." *The Diplomat* (May 25).

 Myers. M. and R. Barrios, 2018. "LAC's Not Part of the Belt and Road, but Does That Matter?" *The Dialogue* (Jan 26).

PART I

Origins of the One Belt One Road Initiative

China's South China Sea Policy:
"Don't Fence Me In"

China's actions in the South China Sea (SCS) are an interesting study in themselves, as well as a potential avenue of exploration through the lens of OBOR/BRI. Under President Xi, China is pursuing a "going out" strategy in an ostensible (provocative, actually) attempt to break what it views as hostile encirclement by the US and its allies. China's activities in the South China Sea are highly visible, "assertive if not aggressive moves." To understand China's behavior in the SCS, it is important to understand the geographic, historical, and economic contexts. Geographically, The People's Republic of China (PRC) technically "shares" the Sea with Cambodia, Brunei, Indonesia, Malaysia, the Philippines, Vietnam, Taiwan, and Thailand. (Lowy Institute, 2018)

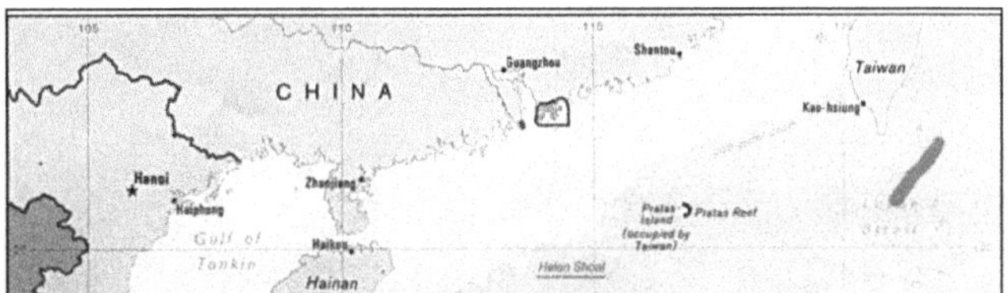

China believes the vast majority of the Sea falls under its sovereign control. With the creation of the PRC in 1949, the Chinese Communist Party issued an a map of the South China Sea with nine dashes, claiming Chinese sovereignty throughout large parts of the sea. The "nine-dash line" has never been officially recognized by the international community, though China continually refers to it, as well as a "ten-dash line," in various claims regarding the sovereignty of the Sea. Other countries bordering the sea such as Vietnam and the Philippines have been vocal, historical opponents to China's SCS policy. The larger of these "foes" in the region would be less likely or less motivated to relinquish their sovereign claims to portions of the sea. Some states at this point in time, e.g., the Philippines, appear to be comfortable relinquishing their legal claims to SCS islands to China, even though the

Fig. 6 Nine-dash line: This is China's demarcation of its perceived sovereign territory. To secure the region, China has laid claim to islands, reefs and sandbars that other nations in the South China Sea also claim as theirs. *Wikipedia.*

International Court of Justice had recently decided in the favor of the Philippines with regard to the Spratly Islands. While various states may occasionally provide different media sound bites and rhetoric to the contrary, the fact is that China is clearly the dominant military power within the Sea. Attempts by states such as the Philippines to militarize within the region have also started to decline in the past year. (Beech, 2018)

As China continues to build up a military presence within the Sea, as well as on the various islands and sea-level reefs located within it, regional neighbors will likely not risk a military engagement with China. Culturally, the Sea is important as it connects China to various "neighbors" in the region. Somewhat ironically, the same natural body of water that has historically allowed for the open exchange of goods and ideas throughout large parts of Asia has become an ongoing source of contention between China and its neighbors, and a future pathway to explore could examine the dynamic between China as a cultural hub and China as a military/political power hub. As China aggressively leans toward the latter, it is most likely that the outer bounds of the Sea will fall under China's 21st Century sphere of influence encompassed by a virtual Great Sea Wall.

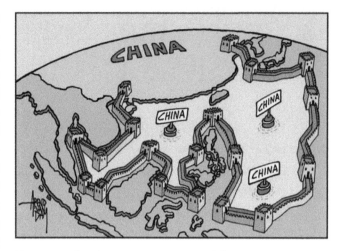

Fig. 7 A political cartoonist's projection of Chinese control over the South China Sea and all things within it! *A. van Dam.*

Understanding the resources and economic components of China's interest in the South China Sea is important because the Sea is critical as a maritime (shipping) gateway, as well as a resource base in itself. The ownership, control and exploitation of the minerals, oil and natural gas, and access to living marine resources are all at stake. Also, massive amounts of these resources, among others, are moved across the Sea's shipping and trade routes. From China's perspective, its perceived sovereignty over the South China Sea, its resources and its shipping lanes, presents a major boon and a stabilizing aspect to its economy. Although China has consistently increased its military dominance within the South China Sea, it has yet to physically block off shipping lanes or major sites of resource extraction for exclusive Chinese use. Should the state begin a campaign of further aggression to maintain or obtain exclusivity in the Sea, significant potential emerges for a "cold-war-like" political atmosphere with the United States and other major powers. Such a Chinese stance could inadvertently result in a "hot" regional military skirmish.

In addition to the factors and talking points described above, the continued development of artificial land masses and military bases within the South China Sea is being closely monitored by several Pacific Rim countries. China's goal with this buildup is likely to claim territory and resources within the Sea, as well as for more strategic and logistical purposes such as maritime and air space control. One of the most notable instances of such a buildup can be seen in the case of Fiery Cross Reef. In the past few years, China has turned the tiny landmass in the Spratly Islands into a functional military operation, complete with a military length runway. (Connor, 2018)

While Philippine officials have stated that China had agreed for years not to militarize the islands, it is clear that vow was broken.

If China continues to militarize and/or construct islands in the SCS, the possibilities are seemingly endless for the state to deploy strategic bases and military/functional operations throughout the Sea. With the state acting seemingly uncontested, that possibility could very well turn into a reality, with vast socioeconomic and geopolitical ramifications for China's neighboring states.

Beyond these startling developments, China has also engaged in a cultural war of sorts via the small contested islands in the Sea. For example, in 2017 China opened a movie theater for the roughly 200 residents of Yongxing (Woody) Island. (Brzeski, 2017) Small developments, such as the construction of a movie theater on a lightly populated island, shed light on the way China views these islands as fully functioning entities that require their own goods and services. As a Chinese media official added "the opening of the cinema is 'part of a plan by local cultural authorities to establish community services on islands under [the regional government's] jurisdiction'." (Brzeski, 2017)

China's actions in the SCS bring to mind the adage that "possession over a property is nine-tenths of the law," meaning that one who has physical control or possession over the property is clearly at an advantage or is in a better position than a person who has no possession over the property. This saying "is not a law but a logical rule of force that has been recognized across ages." (USlegal, n.d.)

China is keen on control of the SCS. In recent times, the US navy as well as Australia have challenged China's self-declared SCS sphere of influence. The Australian government issued a statement about its predicament and its dealings with China. Hill (2016) noted:

The South China Sea disputes have entered a dangerous new phase in the last several years. Alongside China's unprecedented construction and fortification of artificial features, incidents at sea involving clashes between various combinations of fishermen, coast guards and, occasionally, naval assets, are occurring on a routine basis. With the nationalist credentials of authoritarian and dem-ocratically-elected claimant governments at stake, the potential for miscalculation and escalation (whether inadvertent or intended) is growing.

The US has expressed similar concerns about Chinese attempts at harassment of US naval activities in the South China Sea, including the airspace above its SCS artificial islands and bases. For its part, the US continues to hold joint naval exercises with its allies (e.g., UK and Australia) in the Sea as a show of force. For example, Ng and Choi (2019) have reported:

> The United States and Britain have conduct-ed their first joint naval drills in the South China Sea, as Washington seeks support from its allies in challenging Beijing's claim to the disputed waters.

News Flash

A thought-provoking newspaper online headline in the *South China Morning Post* in early February (Wong, 2019) seems to open a new chapter in the South China Sea nine-dash line saga. The headline reads as follows: "Beijing sends fleet of ships to disputed South China Sea island 'to stop the Philippines building facilities.'" The title suggests that there is rising tension in the sea between the Philippines and China. The specific island is named Pagasa (or Zhongye, in Chinese) and the government intends to build a beaching ramp that will enable ships to bring needed supplies to develop the island. The article noted that "Chinese forces have settled into a pattern of monitoring and intimidation after their initial large de-ployment [of numerous civilian and military ships] failed to convince Manila to halt construction."

It was only a few years ago that the Philippines won an ICJ claim against China's take-over (some say out-right occupation) of certain Spratly Islands and reefs. The Chinese government rejected the court's decision and continues to claim and occupy those islands, real and ar-tificial. The Philippines for whatever political reason did not contest China's actions, as long as there would not be a Chinese military buildup on the islands. However, there has now been a military presence, as these islands have dual purpose (civilian and military). One can only wonder if the Philippine government is now regretting its earlier agreement about allowing China's development of the contested SCS islands.

REFERENCES

 Beech, H., 2018. "China's Sea Control is a Done Deal, 'Short of War With the U.S.'" *New York Times* (September 20).

 Brzeski, P., 2017. "China Opens Movie Theater on Politically Contested South China Sea Island." *Hollywood Reporter* (July 23).

 Connor, N., 2018. "China triggers new storm over military build-up on artificial islands." *Telegraph* (January 9).

 Hill, C., 2016. "Australia and the South China Sea: debates and dilemmas" Parliament of Australia, (August).

 Lowy Institute, 2018. "South China Sea" (no date).

 Ng, T. and M. Choi, 2019. "US and British navies carry out first Joint drill in disputed South China Sea." *South China Morning Post* (January 16).

 USlegal, n.d. "Possession is Nine Points of the Law Law and Legal Definition." USlegal.com.

 Wong, C., 2019. "Beijing sends fleet of ships to disputed South China Sea island 'to stop Philippines building facilities'." *South China Morning Post* (February 9).

China's "Going Out" Policy and the Belt and Road Initiative

The Chinese "going out" policy debuted in the late 1980s to enable China's large state-owned enterprises' economic interactions to reach out to the rest of the world. "The Go Out policy is the People's Republic of China's current strategy to encourage its enterprises to invest overseas. Most nations favor attracting inward foreign investment, and support outward foreign investment only passively." (*Wikipedia*, 2017)

In 2013, however, the "going out" policy was taken to a new level, when President Xi rolled out his OBOR Initiative. According to *China Hands* (2017) observers saw Xi's OBOR as starting a new phase, "Going Out 2.0." Domestic economic and political reasons encouraged foreign direct investment (FDI) flowing from China's state-owned enterprises to developing countries through loan-based infrastructure development projects. A major goal included keeping its factories and workers operating at full capacity. Another less obvious but strategic aspect of the "Going Out 2.0" policy has been to expand the acceptance worldwide of the convertibility of China's currency, the RMB or yuan. (Wang, Hongying, 2016)

Several developing countries in which China has already invested through OBOR/BRI face significant safety, stability, transparency and loan-repayment problems. In particular, there is increasing concern by both China and recipient project partners about the ability of the borrowers to re-pay their loans. (Wang Yinwei, 2016) There are examples of what happens when a government, for whatever reason, cannot meet its loan obligations: China's takeover of control and management of infrastructure projects in Sri Lanka and in Zambia. Nevertheless, Xi's "One Belt One Road" continues to appeal to leaders of countries in Asia, the Middle East, Africa, South, Southeastern, Eastern, Central and Western Europe, and now Latin America.

While China continues to pursue "going out," complaints from existing OBOR/BRI partners may make prospective partners more reluctant to allow Chinese investments to "come in," as enticing as Chinese loan arrangements for desired infrastructure might be.

The ascendency of Xi Jinping to the presidency of China in 2013, following his predecessor President Hu Jintao, could be marked as an apparent beginning of a sea change in China's domestic and foreign policies. Instead of being content with favorable trade balances with the US and other trading partners, President Xi chose to pursue a strategic shift in its international policy from one of self-imposed restraint to one of aggressively "going out," which meant becoming an active global player politically and economically as well as militarily.

Fast & Furious, the title of various fictitious Hollywood movies since the 1970s, could serve as a more descriptive subtitle of China's OBOR Initiative. Since its introduction in late 2013, it has seen nothing short of a meteoric rise in interest by scores of country leaders, not only in the regions noted above, but also, more recently, around the globe. It is the phoenix-like rebirth of the myth-and-fact-laden ancient Silk Road in the form of a modern-day New Economic Silk Road.

Interest in OBOR has sparked trade and infrastructure activities over the past five years that had taken decades to centuries to develop in earlier times. OBOR activities in the form of memos of understanding and formal bilateral agreements have been appearing in the news monthly, if not weekly, as China pursued partners in the construction of infrastructure projects through seemingly advantageous loans to willing countries. Hundreds of billions of US dollars in loans have already been planned or expended through President Xi's flagship OBOR Initiative.

China has been on a learning curve with regard to "going out," through its many OBOR/BRI development initiatives based ostensibly on the infrastructure needs and wants of developing and graduated developing countries. China's rapid economic development in the past few decades, and now its status as the richest developing country, have inspired other developing countries to mimic China's development successes through China's willingness to provide loans they would not so easily get from Western institutions. Western countries such as the

United States, Japan, Korea and the Europe Union, are only recently showing signs of serious concern about the adverse political and economic implications of the growth of Chinese loan arrangements, infrastructure and trade projects, as well as of the spreading political, even military, influence in countries belatedly deemed important to their collective security. Of these Western countries, the United States appears to have been among the last to show commensurate interest in, or concern about, China's OBOR/BRI.

US political interest in China's OBOR/BRI began to go public with Congressional and National Intelligence hearings in November 2017. *NDTV* (2017), an Indian news channel, reported that in a hearing of the US House Foreign Affairs Subcommittee on Asia and the Pacific, a congressman succinctly captured America's rising concern:

The Belt and Road projects are financed by Chinese institutions at high [interest] rates (not typically found in the development context) by Chinese corporations that are often state-owned enterprises and utilize Chinese labour and material and seem to add little to local economies and bring unsustainable debt burdens.

A development expert at the hearings added, "China has displayed willingness to 'periodically overlook human rights, environmental or social standards' in the way that it approaches development." This perspective is important to remember, as we consider OBOR/BRI development internationally.

REFERENCES

 China Hands, 2017. "China 'Going Out' 2.0: Dawn of a New Era for Chinese Investment Abroad." *Huffington Post* (December 6).

 NDTV, 2017. "China's Belt And Road Project 'More Than What Meets The Eye': US Lawmakers." (November 21).

 Wang, Hongying, 2016. "A deeper look at China's 'going out' policy." *CIGI Commentary* (March 8).

Wang, Yiwei. 2016. *The Belt and Road Initiative: What will China offer the world in its rise.* Reprinted 2018. (Beijing, China: New World Press). ISBN 978-7510455537.

 Wikipedia, 2017. "Go Out Policy." (October 30).

The Power of "One": The 2008 Beijing Olympics

In January 2005 the Chinese government initiated a contest to select the slogan and image for its 2008 Beijing Olympics. The winning slogan, selected from more than 100,000 entries, was "One World One Dream." Once the slogan had been selected, Liu Qi, President of the Beijing Organizing Committee for the XXIX Olympiad (BOCOG), said in an official press release in the *China Daily* (Lei, 2005) that "One World One Dream" "is a slogan that conveys the lofty ideal of people in Beijing as well as in China…" and "It expresses the firm belief of a great nation, with a long history of 5,000 years and on its way towards modernization, that it is committed to peaceful development, a harmonious society and people's happiness."

The official program for the opening ceremony (on 08/08/2008) succinctly described the slogan in the following way: "One World. One Dream. You and me, we are of one family; You and me, we are creating a bright future."

Again, Lei (2005) noted, "The English translation of the slogan is distinctive in sentence structure. The two 'ones' are perfectly used in parallel, and the words 'World' and 'Dream' form a good match. The slogan is simple, meaningful, inspiring, and easy to remember, read and spread."

In this regard, a remark by a European reporter is worthy of note: "The slogan sounds very good," said an Italian journalist covering the ceremony. "It conveys the wish of Chinese people to join the world."

At first reading, this appears as an attempt by a *China Daily* writer to add foreign praise about the newly released Olympic slogan. However, in retrospect the comment may have captured the true underlying value to China of hosting the 29th Olympic Games. It was an expression of China's opening up (i.e., "going out") to the world in a new and more engaging way than had been the case since 1949 when the Communist regime came to power.

Clearly the Olympic theme was well received inside China as well as outside. Quoting Liu again, "We belong to the same world and we share the same aspirations and dreams." In 2005 and through the Olympics, China's current President Xi was a high-level figure in the Chinese

Fig. 8 Participation medal for athletes in the 2008 Olympics. Did the Beijing Olympic slogan influence the naming of OBOR? *Xiao Yong, Olympic Museum.*

Communist Party and government, and was the designated successor to then-President Hu Jintao. What we are speculating here is that the success of the One World One Dream slogan (viewed as a brand) inspired the development of President Xi's naming of the One Belt One Road Initiative. It also emphasized reasons behind the success of the Beijing Olympics slogan. As Liu stated, the Olympic slogan "voices the aspirations of 1.3 billion Chinese people to contribute to the establishment of a peaceful and bright world."

A common concern raised by other countries that might partner with China was as follows: what is meant by the use of the word "one" in OBOR. Did it mean China would treat each partner as an equal in their financial arrangements? Or, did it mean that there would be only "one" way to develop economically in the future, the Chinese way? This sentiment was well captured in the following political cartoon shown on the next page.

The gestures and concerns raised about the meaning of "one" were apparently frequent enough to pressure Chinese authorities to re-brand OBOR. Official reasons for dropping the word "one" included the following: wordsmithing (to avoid misinterpretations), image modification (so China would not appear to be a regional or global hegemon) or action-oriented (to show China operates "apolitically" and, therefore, differently than Western governments and their institutions).

The word "one" had become a non-trivial concern to other economies that were interested in considering an OBOR partnership with China. To reduce any misunderstandings about China's motives behind the Initiative, OBOR was officially re-named in 2015 as the "Belt and Road Initiative" (BRI) in accordance with the following official instructions:

Fig. 9   Note that the only one in the car wearing a seatbelt is the driver. *Sinann.*

1. In all the official documents, the official translation should be "the Silk Road Economic Belt and the 21st-Century Maritime Silk Road" and for short it is "the Belt and Road", the abbreviation is "B&R";
2. Using initiative, not "strategy," "project," "program," "agenda";
3. Due to the popularity of OBOR, in unofficial situations, after the first time using the full translation, i.e., "the Silk Road Economic Belt and the 21st-Century Maritime Silk Road", other short names such as "the Belt and Road initiative" and/or "the land and maritime Silk Road initiative" can be used. No other translation should be used. (My Drivers, 2015)

Despite the best efforts of Chinese officials to abruptly stop by decree the use of the OBOR acronym, the apparent eye-catching, rhythmic OBOR brand has proven difficult to erase. As a result, One Belt One Road and its acronym, OBOR, are still frequently used in the popular media, even within articles that refer primarily to BRI.

When OBOR's name was changed to BRI, an Eastern European news headline noted, "BRI Instead of OBOR – China Edits the English Name of its Most Ambitious International Project." This article suggested China's key reason for re-branding the initiative:

China has sacrificed a catchy, trending brand name [e.g., OBOR], which has become widely recognized within both traditional and social media, as well as the professional circles, out of fear of being misunderstood. (LIIA, 2016)

The Chinese agency that rebranded OBOR to BRI, however, was apparently unaware of the power of a brand and of brand loyalty. The OBOR brand had already taken hold in the media in a very short time. Had the Chinese agency responsible for the official re-branding of the OBOR been familiar with the literature on branding products, they might have modified the name while retaining the original OBOR acronym. An interesting review of failed attempts at changing brands of popular consumer products suggested that once a brand becomes popular, it no longer belongs to the company (in this case the country, China). It belongs to the consumers of the product, as a result of brand loyalty. (Haoues, 2015)

Although the name of the initiative was officially changed, the meaning of the "one" (viewed as China-centric) continues to arise in critiques of the BRI. In sum, the success of the One World One Dream slogan may not have transferred as well as intended to the OBOR Initiative. Governments still wonder about China's long-term underlying intentions about the BRI.

"Since Xi Jinping came to power in 2012, he had been promoting a significant shift within Chinese politics under a new and catchy label: the China Dream." (Fasulo, 2016) Fasulo then presented an interesting brief historical perspective on Xi's political use of the concept of "dream" as a traditional Chinese slogan. He suggested that Xi's "China Dream promises the modernization of China by the middle of the 21st Century and is aimed at giving back the prominent international role that China lost after the First Opium War [1839-42]".

The reference to the mid-21st Century is actually about assuring China's global superpower status by the time of the 100th anniversary in 2049 of the victory of the Communist establishment of the People's Republic of China.

REFERENCES

 Fasulo, F., 2016. "Waking from the China Dream" (Chapter 1). In A. Amighini (Ed.), *China Dream: Still Coming True?* (Milan, Italy: ISPI).

 Haoues, R., 2015. "30 years ago today, Coca-Cola made its worst mistake." *CBS Evening News* (April 23).

 Lei, L., 2005. "Beijing 2008 Games: One World, One Dream." *China Daily* (Updated: June 27).

 LIIA, 2016. "一带一路"官方英译公布：简称 BRI Instead of OBOR – China Edits the English Name of its Most Ambitious International Project" Latvian Institute of International Affairs (July 28).

 My Drivers, 2015. "B&R" [The official English translation of the "Belt and Road" announcement: Abbreviation B&R]. (September 24).

China's New Economic and Maritime Silk Roads and Belts

At first, President Xi's invoking of the symbol and spirit of the ancient Silk Road suggested to many observers a rekindling of a romanticized bygone era, a view of Chinese history that was more in line with a Marco Polo journey than a modernized China on a path to spread its influence across the Eurasian landmass to Europe, the Middle East and Northeastern Africa. However, as Zhang (2015) reported, "it is a misunderstanding that China acts out of nostalgia in pursuing this initiative…. While the new initiative follows an old path, the Silk Road, it is anything but nostalgic." Images of camel trains cutting across harsh deserts and mountainous terrain centuries ago have been replaced today by high-speed rail lines, highways, oil and gas pipelines, deep-water ports and energy grids.

Quoting a recent statement by a German Foreign Minister with a skeptical view of the motives behind the Silk Road Initiative, Miller (2018) wrote "The initiative for a new Silk Road is not – as some in Germany believe – a sentimental reminder of Marco Polo. Rather…it is no longer just about the economy: China is developing a comprehensive system alternative to the Western one, which, unlike our model, is not based on freedom, democracy and individual human rights."

When OBOR was first launched, its six original roads and belts might have been viewed by outsiders as just bringing together, under one over-arching government program, new, in-progress and existing Chinese foreign commer-

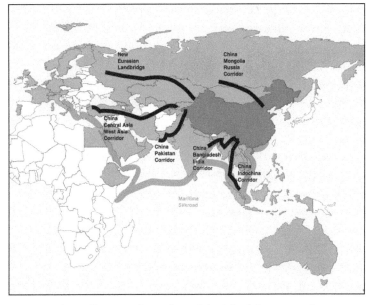

Fig. 10   Shows China in red, members of the Asian Infrastructure Investment Bank in orange, Maritime routes in blue and the six corridors of OBOR in black. Lommes, *Wikipedia*.

Fig. 11   Existing infrastructure projects were put under the OBOR umbrella along with new projects undertaken after the launching of OBOR in 2013. *CCB*.

cial infrastructure-related bilateral ventures.

Skeptics remind us of an old adage about "putting old wine in a new bottle," e.g., business-as-usual but under a new name. For example, one researcher, quoted in Craw (2017), suggested "while Chinese President Xi Jinping's 2013 speech on the [OBOR] plan has seen it hyped as a 'new strategy,' it's actually a 'continuation' of an old idea to assert Chinese political and economic power." As "business-as-usual" as OBOR may have seemed at first, it has proven to be anything but that. "As the notion of a modern Silk Road gained traction, Belt and Road meandered into places that had never had any connection with ancient caravans. This year it reached South America, the Caribbean, and even the Arctic. In June, it rocketed into space." (Majendie *et al.*, 2018) The initiative inspired the marketing of new China-centric development opportunities that surprised Western Powers. (Rosen, 2018) The adjacent graphic highlights OBOR news headlines. Similar headlines can be found using "Belt and Road Initiative" as the key Internet search phrase.

Retiring German Foreign Minister Sigmar Gabriel remarked in his

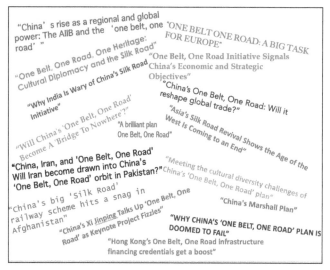

Fig. 12 OBOR Headlines pro and con, as of May 2018. *CCB.*

farewell speech that China is "currently the only country in the world with a truly global, geo-strategic idea." He warned that "it is not in the interest of democracy or freedom, and that the West needs to offer an alternative…." He said "China was using its $5 trillion USD One Belt One Road (OBOR) infrastructure fund to promote a value system different from the West." (Miller, 2018)

"Geographically, OBOR could span 65 countries responsible for roughly 70 percent of the world's population. Economically, it could include Chinese investments approaching $4 trillion." (Wang Yiwei, 2016) The initiative was open to worldwide cooperation, including Western countries. Heffernan (2017) noted, "It covers, but is not limited to, the area of the ancient Silk Road. It is open to all countries, and international and regional organizations for engagement, so that the results of the concerted efforts will benefit wider areas."

Harper (2017) reported that "The image of the Silk Road has been reinforced by Xi Jinping's utilization of China's imperial past as a source of national pride, promoting the idea of a 'Chinese' global order to fill the vacuum left by the protectionism and isolationism of the Trump administration." Tang and Wong (2016) had noted a year earlier, "At a time when established world powers are struggling with domestic problems, Xi sees a

chance to push ahead with his oddly worded brainchild [OBOR], a geopolitical push to extend Beijing's influence to remote corners of the globe."

Within China, Xi called on (i.e., strongly encouraged) his government ministries and agencies, provinces, cities and companies to be involved in OBOR/BRI. Outside observers suggested that a major catalyst for the infrastructure initiative was a need to address China's domestic problems. As one example, Gautrin (2018) identified some of those domestic benefits:

The BRI is a clear win-win initiative for the PRC. It comes at an opportune time for the country. Supporting large infrastructure projects abroad would help resolve the overcapacity problems for both cement and steel. (Miller, 2018) In addition, infrastructure, and more specifically transport infrastructure, has always been a major contributor to economic growth, and the initiative presents a new opportunity.

More specifically,

The expansion of the Eurasian land bridge is bringing a new era of prosperity to the centers of production in central PRC to cities like Chongqing, Chengdu, and Xian. The BRI is also used as an instrument to foster growth in peripheral provinces like Xinjiang, Yunnan, and Guangxi and to revive growth in the northeast. In fact, all provinces have been asked under the BRI to prepare qualifying infrastructure projects.

REFERENCES

 Craw, V., 2017. China's Belt and Road Initiative could redraw the map on global trade." (July 23).

 Gautrin, J., 2018. "One Belt One Road and the Risks Behind the Win-Win Situation." *Asia Pathways*. Blog of the Asia Development Bank Institute (March 5).

 Harper, T., 2017. "BRI and the New Great Game in Eurasia." *Asia Dialogue* (November 29).

 Heffernan, J., 2017. "Inside the China's Belt and Road Initiative." (May 19).

 Majendie, A. *et al.*, 2018. "China's Empire of Money Is Reshaping Global Trade." *Bloomberg News* (August 1).

 Miller, N., 2018. China undermining us 'with stick and carrots': Outgoing German Minister." *The Sydney Morning Herald* (February 19).

 Rosen, S., 2018. "Xi Jinping's grasp on power has captured the West's attention – now what?" *The Conversation* (March 3).

 Tang, F. and C. Wong, 2016. "As Trump retreats, Xi Jinping moves to upgrade China's global power play." *South China Morning Post* (December 2).

Wang, Yiwei., 2016. *The Belt and Road Initiative: What will China offer the world in its rise*. Reprinted 2018. (Beijing, China: New World Press). ISBN 978-7510455537.

 Zhang, L., 2015. "One Belt, One Road – An Old but Non-Nostalgic Path," Vol.2 (2): 225-227. (April 28).

The Geopolitics of OBOR/BRI

China is on its way to creating a new *de facto* Asia-based geopolitical World Order that is already beginning to challenge the dominance of Western development agencies as well as their governments.

Early in the life of OBOR/BRI, Huang (2016) suggested that:

> Compared with other forms of international economic cooperation such as WTO and G20, the Belt & Road Initiative is open in nature and does not exclude any interested parties. Chinese officials explicitly said that countries like Japan and Korea are welcome to participate in the initiative. And the market-based rule means that, while the Initiative was a policy proposal, implementation of it has to make commercial sense. It is not international aid by the Chinese government. (p. 318)

By 2018, OBOR/BRI had taken on a higher level of geopolitical importance to China and had become a major concern to some Western powers, especially the US. President Xi's centerpiece policy seemingly was designed to "Make China's 'Silk Road' Great Again." However, it has far surpassed the spirit of the ancient Silk Road. In retrospect, however, that may not have been Xi's longer-term strategic intention. Officially, OBOR/BRI is scheduled to end in 2049, which will be the 100th anniversary of the establishment of the People's Republic of China.

LeVine (2015) noted that "China is building the most extensive global commercial-military empire in history." Through OBOR/BRI, China is set to travel the pathways toward empire as did the Romans and later, the British. Shi (2018) correctly observed that "the sun never sets on China's trade and infrastructure ambition. With the addition of the Arctic and Latin America last week, Chinese President Xi Jinping's signature Belt and Road Initiative has become truly global." The OBOR/BRI network now encircles the globe.

Hillman (2016) offered a cautionary observation:

> Infrastructure projects, therefore, can be important windows into national interests and ambitions.

History urges caution. Last century's infrastructure projects created new economic opportunities, reshaped relationships within and between states, and even served as catalysts of, and instruments for, war. As the world's economic center of gravity moves east, today's projects [e.g., OBOR/BRI] could preview a new order that is emerging.

For decades, China has been involved in bilateral projects internationally with various targeted countries by constructing dams, pipelines, roads, railroads and airports and rehabilitating aging infrastructure such as ports and bridges. The difference now is that, under the OBOR/BRI brand, China's activities are viewed as more multinational, seemingly more transparent, more focused, more coordinated and working toward making China a world political force. Despite its official pronouncements to the contrary, it is no longer just a global economic influence and political power: it has already become a military power to be reckoned with.

At the risk of overstating the influence of OBOR's success on President Xi's more assertive stance toward the West and soft power toward its Asian neighbors and other OBOR/BRI partners in Africa as well, it is interesting to point out the role reversals between the major protagonists of the West and the East, the US and China, respectively, as suggested by Di Lieto (2018):

> China's goal is to use the Regional Comprehensive Economic Partnership (RCEP) negotiations to accelerate its major Asian infrastructure projects. The most notable of these are the Belt and Road Initiative and the Asian Infrastructure Investment Bank. This initiative promises to compete with the Western-centric World Bank and [the] Japan-led Asian Development Bank.
>
> It's not an arms race, but infrastructure projects, investments and even humanitarian aid that are

fueling Xi's "major-power diplomacy with Chinese characteristics." This means clusters of Asian countries are becoming more and more embedded in China's economic and strategic policy.

Strangely, Trump's strategic triangle is making US policy look like China's after it opened to the global economy in the 1980s. Conversely, Xi Jinping's more assertive regional politics is moving China to where the US was before Trump – with defense on top of trade and industry.

In the 2016 US presidential election, both candidates – Trump and Clinton – opposed US participation in TPP (Trans-Pacific Partnership). When Trump became president, he withdrew the US from the TPP, an agreement that President Obama had been fostering. This presented an opportunity for China to pursue its regional trade agreement, RCEP. AFP (2018) wrote that RCEP, "covering half the world's population, is billed as an antidote to Donald Trump's 'America First.'" AFP went on to note "trade diplomats…indicated negotiation on the RCEP, a sweeping 16-country deal that includes China, Japan, India and the 10 members of the Southeast Asian Nations, will carry on deep into 2019…. RCEP is now the world's biggest trade deal."

One example of China's early attempts to demonstrate its technological capabilities was its highly-publicized launching of a 16-day freight train service from Yiwu in eastern China to England. The significance of this at first was more of symbolic nature than of commercial trade value. Yet, aside from any commercial benefits that might accrue to China and to England, geopolitical benefits appeared large. Gramer (2017) raised the following political aspects:

China's railway from the Pacific to London showcases the country's turn toward Europe at a time of tension with the United States. The Yiwu-London line lays bare the geopolitical ambitions underpinning China's [OBOR/BRI] policy….

Until recently a US ambition to help bring security to Central Asia, this "New Silk Road" could take on even more importance if the US-China trade relationship goes south, as early and hawkish postures by President-elect Trump and his team have indicated.

Those on the receiving end are thrilled at what the new rail services could offer, especially corners of Europe that still lag economically…. Chinese

investment in energy projects, railroads, and port facilities in Europe and around the rim of the Indian Ocean may pay bigger geopolitical dividends than economic returns.

Why Yiwu? It is important to note that the Chinese on the shipping end of the Yiwu-to-London rail line are also ecstatic for economic reasons. *Bloomberg News* (2018a) reported that Yiwu, a couple hours from Shanghai, a city of 1.2 million people, got a big boost from the Belt and Road Initiative. This article mentioned that "The first Europe-bound train pulled out of here in November 2014, heading to Kazakhstan and Russia, then through Eastern Europe and on to Madrid…. Since then more routes have opened to destinations including London, Amsterdam, and Tehran." It noted that the market of Yiwu "is unlike any other: A vast complex…across an expanse the size of 650 soccer fields."

Having captured international attention through OBOR/BRI, it appears that Xi is now openly striving to make China one of the foremost 21st Century trade, large-scale construction and commercial centers worldwide by 2025.

There has been increasing news coverage about China's military since the buildup of military activity on artificial islands and reefs in the South China Sea earlier this decade. China claims these are defensive moves to protect its claims within its self-declared nine-dash line in the SCS. Yet signs are appearing that suggest otherwise. For example, China has established a military base in Djibouti.

In the first few days of 2019, Jun (2019) reported the "Hundreds of senior officials from all provinces and autonomous regions were summoned to Beijing for a Communist Party study on risk control." In his opening address, President Xi told them, "Take all necessary precautionary steps and be vigilant about any risks that could jeopardise China's stability and reforms." Jun quoted Xi:

[We are] confronted with unpredictable international developments and a complicated and sensitive external environment [a phrase invoked by Chinese leaders to refer to rising threats from China's trade war with Washington].

We must keep our high alert about any "black swan" [or unforeseen] incident, and also take steps to prevent any "grey rhino" [highly possible yet ignored threats].

To be sure, Xi's concerns were in large measure related to the US attacks on China in general and more specifically on its trade-war with China, on alleged industrial espionage (e.g., Huawei), on China's SCS policy and on its "Made in China 2025" campaign.

Xi also said that "[We] must complete a security system for the "Belt and Road Initiative." That involves the opening for China to provide security for protection of the construction and, later, protection of their infrastructure projects outside of the country. There has already been a growth in "private" security firms in China as well and, in some cases, China has offered military troop support to protect its infrastructure projects and its overseas workers.

Xi's calls for vigilance come at a time that Chinese authorities are reducing the size of the ground forces of the PLA. However, the four other military branches – navy, air force, rocket force and strategic force – are being expanded, modernized and shifting to high-tech for a future-oriented 21st century military establishment. One political observer referred to China as a "stealth superpower." (Mastro, 2019)

REFERENCES

 AFP, 2018. "China-backed RCEP trade deal pushed back to 2019." *Bangkok Post* (November 13).

 Bloomberg News, 2018a. "China's Empire of Money Is Reshaping Global Trade." (August 1).

 Di Lieto, G., 2018. "In the power struggle for Asia, Trump and Xi Jinping are switching policies." *Asia Dialogue* (January 25).

 Gramer, R., 2017. "All Aboard China's 'New Silk Road' Express." *Foreign Policy* (January 4).

 Hillman, J., 2016. "OBOR on the Ground: Evaluating China's 'One Belt, One Road' Initiative at the Project Level." Presented at the US Naval War College Workshop on China's Silk Road Initiative. (November 30).

 Huang, Y., 2016. "Understanding China's Belt & Road Initiative: Motivation, framework and assessment." *China Economic Review*, Issue 40 (September) pp. 314-321.

 Jun, M., 2019. "Be vigilant about threats to China's stability and reforms, Xi Jinping tells top cadre." *South China Morning Post* (January 22).

 LeVine, S., 2015. "China is building the most extensive global commercial-military empire in history." *Quartz* (June 9).

 Mastro, O.S., 2019. "The Stealth Superpower: How China Hid Its Global Ambitions." *Foreign Affairs* (January-February).

 Shi, T., 2018. "China's Infrastructure Push Reaches Arctic, Leaving out the U.S." *Bloomberg Quint* (January 29).

"Made in China 2025" and the US

Ever since 2013, when Xi Jinping became China's President, China's "going out" policy reached a new level of intensity. Xi launched his OBOR Initiative in 2013 to provide loans to developing countries for infrastructure development projects. Currently, about 70 countries are partnering with China in such development projects. In 2015 Xi's "Made in China 2025" (MIC 2025) was launched as a domestic campaign. One could argue that, with regard to its importance as a domestic economic development objective, it is second only to the One Belt One Road Initiative.

What MIC 2025 Is

McBride (2018) reported that MIC 2025 "is the government's ten-year plan to update China's manufacturing base by rapidly developing ten high-tech industries. Chief among these are electric cars and other new energy vehicles, next generation information technology (IT) and telecommunications, and advanced robotics and artificial intelligence."

The adjacent image is the cover of the U.S. Chamber of Commerce (2017) report which highlights the various high-tech industries for which China hopes to fast-track their competitive edge with established industrial countries.

Cyrill (2018) noted that the MIC 2025 plan was designed to shift the country "from being a low-end manufacturer to becoming a high-end producer of goods." *Bloomberg News* (2018b) commented on China's rationale:

As its economy transitions away from labor-intensive industries – like clothing and footwear manufacture – China views its shift into higher-tech

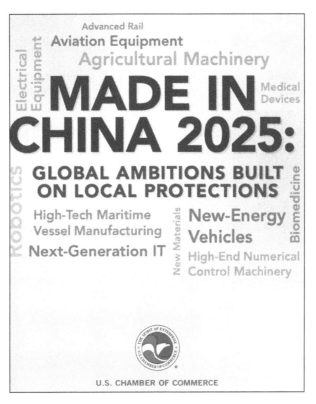

Fig. 13   The Made in China 2025 plan has become a central US concern in its 2018-19 trade war with China. *U.S. Chamber of Commerce.*

manufacturing as a crucial part of its development. Labor costs are surging as the rapidly aging population causes the workforce to shrink, undermining competitiveness in sweatshop industries that underpinned its rise. To thrive, China must shift into industries now dominated by developed economies.

This involved rapidly upgrading, modernizing and acquiring high-tech manufacturing to compete with the already industrialized countries such as the US, Japan, South Korea, and countries in the European Union.

Wübbeke *et al.* (2016) reported that:

China's ambitious plan [is] to build one of the world's most advanced and competitive economies with the help of innovative manufacturing technologies ("smart manufacturing"). The Plan aims to turn the country into a "manufacturing superpower" over the coming decades.... The strategy targets virtually all high-tech industries that strongly contribute to economic growth in advanced economies.

McBride also noted:

> The program aims to use government subsidies, mobilize state-owned enterprises [SOEs] and pursue intellectual property acquisition to catch up with – and then surpass – Western technological prowess in advanced industries.

What MIC 2025 Does

MIC 2025 was designed to "leapfrog" the industrialization progress of the West by focusing on the development of smart industry using government subsidies. Leapfrogging is defined as "an advance from one place, position, or situation to another without progressing through all or any of the places or stages in between."

China set specific limits for the percentage of imported components of China's export products and targets for those projected percentages: by 2020 high-tech product components are to be 40% made in China, by 2025 it is to be 70%, and by 2049, 100%. This is seen by China as economic development, and by other countries as an economic threat. (e.g., Wübekke et al., 2016)

How MIC 2025 Does It

A key, fast-track approach to upgrading China's capabilities with smart manufacturing (e.g., smart phones, chips, artificial intelligence, robotics) would require the acquisition of foreign hi-tech enterprises. By 2018 this raised the concern of European governments and the attention of the United States.

Wübbeke *et al.* (2016, pp. 7-8) went on to write:

> China's technology acquisitions are partly supported and guided by the state. China pursues an outbound

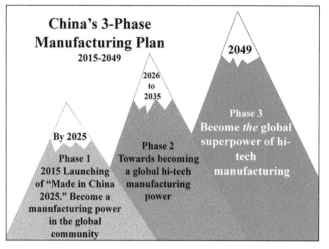

Fig. 14 The Made in China 2025 plan is just the first of three phases extending to 2049. *CCB. Adapted from J. Wu.*

Recent Headlines about MIC 2025

- How 'Made in China 2025' became a lightning rod in 'war over China's national destiny'
- 'Made in China 2025': is Beijing's plan for hi-tech dominance as big a threat as the West thinks it is?
- "Made In China 2025" Master Plan Has Hit a Wall Named Trump
- Foreign Firms Wary Of 'Made In China 2025,' But It May Be China's Best Chance At Innovation
- How 'Made in China 2025' Frames Trump's Trade Threats
- Why Made in China 2025 Will Succeed, Despite Trump
- Beijing eases back on "Made in China 2025" amid trade talks with U.S.
- Beijing drops contentious 'Made in China 2025' slogan but policy remains

industrial policy with government capital and highly opaque investor networks to facilitate high-tech acquisitions abroad.

China has been interacting with other trading partners on an uneven playing field that favored China: China could freely invest in market-driven economies while at the same time protecting its own industries from foreign ownership.

US/Trump Initial Lack of Concern

When Donald Trump was running for US president in 2016 and later as President, he made it very clear that he did not believe in soft power (e.g., multilateral diplomacy or foreign aid). He opposed globalization and favored bilateral negotiations to address trade imbalances and practices, which he believed were a threat to American interests.

One of Trump's first decisions was to seek to cut the budgets of the State Department and of the US Agency for International Development (USAID) by roughly 35 percent. The US Congress avoided making such draconian cuts, but the President's attitude toward humanitarian and other foreign assistance remained toxic: "He vowed to 'stop sending aid to countries that hate us'" (Thrush, 2018).

Initially, little attention by the media seems to have been paid to MIC 2025. The US was late to take the growing economic and geopolitical influence of Xi's China seriously. A news report (*Bloomberg News*, 2018b) entitled "How 'Made in China 2025' Frames Trump's Trade Threats" presented the following comment on April 10 that has now linked Trump's trade war with the "Made in China 2025" campaign:

A plan called "Made in China 2025" is generating more attention now than when the Chinese government first announced it in 2015. In short, it's a blueprint for transforming the country into an advanced manufacturing economy. So, why the sudden interest? Look no further than U.S. President Donald Trump's threat to impose trade tariffs on Chinese imports.

US Responds

The US belatedly responded to Xi's MIC 2025 with a policy to compete with China's infrastructure initiative in the developing world, although China had been pursuing an accelerated "going out" policy for the past five or so years. In early October, Thrush (2018) reported that:

President Trump, seeking to counter China's growing geopolitical influence, is embracing a major expansion of foreign aid that will bankroll infrastructure projects in Africa, Asia and the Americas – throwing his support behind an initiative he once sought to scuttle.

The bill, entitled "Better Utilization of Investments Leading to Development (BUILD) Act" created a new $60 billion USD aid agency called the US International Development Finance Corporation (IDFC).

As suggested by Thrush, "the president's shift has less to do with a sudden embrace of foreign aid than a desire to block Beijing's plan for economic, technological and political dominance." The law was designed to limit China's ability to acquire certain high-tech businesses deemed to be strategic for national security.

The US law was clearly a late response to China's OBOR, which is now perceived as a threat to the West along with its MIC 2025 plan (see also Pilling and Politi's 2018 article entitled "US senate passes $60bn foreign development bill"; Jaipragas, 2018).

This political US response was an attempt to counter the growing influence of Chinese infrastructure development activities and took place during the early months of the Trump-initiated trade war with China.

Saldinger (2018) described the three-year process that led to BUILD:

With the National Security Strategy and the budget, two of the key arguments in favor of the [BUILD] proposal emerged: It was an effort to counter China

and would make the US more competitive abroad. [According to a Senior White House Official], "The national security perspective is very important for us to promote US ideals, free markets, business-led investment. It's important for us that China doesn't occupy all of this space and lead countries to investments that aren't good for them." The official also commented that "the White House was looking for a way to promote economic development and provide an alternative to the financing China was providing through the Belt and Road Initiative."

China's Reaction to the US Reaction

As concerned as Chinese authorities had become about adverse international reaction to their use of the word "One" in the One Belt One Road Initiative – a concern that led to the initiative's name being officially changed to the Belt and Road Initiative – it is paralleled in how they have become concerned about international reaction to their MIC 2025 campaign. Industrialized countries saw it as a strategic Chinese challenge to their economies by creating Chinese home-grown (or foreign-acquired) high-tech industries by the year 2049.

CNBC (2018) reported that as a result of US concern, it appears that publicizing its MIC 2025 objective has been officially curtailed. Chinese leaders realize they may have tactically erred by raising too much awareness about China's fast-track attempt to close a gap with America and Europe in high technology manufacturing capabilities, especially by 2025.

Trivedi (2018) wrote that:

Beijing is considering delaying targets in its "Made in China 2025" program…. The roadmap, which seeks to advance domestic production of critical technology, has been a key bone of contention in President Donald Trump's trade war. Other reports said China may replace the program altogether and give foreign companies more access to its market.

A major concern for the US Government and other countries as well has been China's illegal industrial espionage activities and its theft, illegal use or acquisition of intellectual property. China has been caught in the past in attempts to steal US technology secrets and industrial innovations. *Bloomberg News* (2018b) stated US concerns this way:

U.S. companies have long argued that China uses a range of tactics to force them to transfer intellectual property such as industrial designs and patents, and that Chinese entities engage in widespread theft of U.S. trade secrets. Foreign companies fear they won't be able to compete against Chinese companies in advanced manufacturing when they are backed by massive state investment and subsidies.

US Claims Against China

While the "Made in China 2025" slogan highlights China's plan and timetable to compete effectively with Western industrial nations in high-tech fields such as robotics, aerospace technology, and artificial intelligence, it takes on a different meaning for those Western powers worried about their intellectual property rights. Allegations of industrial theft as well as the coerced turnover of high-tech secrets to Chinese firms in order for foreign firms to operate in Chinese joint ventures are associated with the MIC 2025 modernization effort. For example, most recently, such allegations centered on the theft of plans for an aircraft engine in an attempt to create a Chinese competitor in the commercial aeronautic industry.

Bloomberg News (2018c) reported on the linking of the MIC 2025 brand to the US-China trade war in its article, "The U.S. Ratchets Up Fight Over 'China 2025' by Accusing Chinese Spies of a Plot to Steal Jet Engine Tech:"

> Beijing's Made in China 2025 blueprint specifically identifies aerospace as a key sector that can help match or exceed the high-end manufacturing output of countries such as Germany, Japan and the U.S. Trump administration demands that China roll back support for the plan have been a major sticking [point] in discussions to resolve [their] trade dispute.

Although China may tone down in public the use of "Made in China 2025" or openly profess in international forums to have dropped that campaign or motivational slogan, It will in no way give up striving to become a highly competitive manufacturing superpower.

A Way Out for China?

One way to circumvent the current or future trade wars with the US would be for Chinese companies to move their factories to countries in Southeast Asia. A recent Hong Kong article (HKTDC 2019) has made such a suggestion. The article, entitled "Made in China Moves to Indonesia," lays out favorable reasons to pursue such a strategy that can "cut costs and navigate around obstacles created by the Sino-US trade dispute." The article noted:

> One option is to take production lines offshore. The cost-effectiveness of wages in these offshore centers [such as India, Indonesia and Vietnam] is an important consideration.

According to a report in *Bloomberg Quint* (2018):

> …the U.S. now sees China as a strategic rival and imposing such curbs would mark a concrete shift in its strategy toward containing China's ascent in advanced industries. By way of an escalating US-initiated trade war with China, it is not realistic on the part of President Trump to expect China to surrender its sovereign right to develop high-tech manufacturing. China will, more sooner than later, compete effectively with the US and other industrialized nations in the realm of high-tech manufacturing."

News Flash

Klein and Delaneny (2019) reported on the latest US response to "Made in China 2025:"

> China faces a tougher fight in its standoff with Washington after calls to counter Beijing's global ambitions gained momentum in the US capital mounted on Tuesday [February 13]. Republican Senator Marco Rubio proposed legislation that would restrict and tax Chinese investments in the US to counter Beijing's "Made in China 2025" (MIC 2025) industrial modernization programme, which includes direct subsidies for domestic companies developing advanced semiconductors.

Published on the same day as Senator Rubio's announcement above, Valencia (2019) takes a different approach to a possible rapprochement between the US and China. Commenting on the recently-proposed US strategic approach of 'competitive coexistence,' Valencia wrote, "the US must accept China's growing influence and realistically negotiate the transition to a new order in which power is shared." He suggested that the US approach would be a "fool's errand," providing the following reasons in his article's concluding paragraph.

Indeed, the thinking behind the proposal for "competitive coexistence" is a good indication of why US policy towards China has "failed" and probably will continue to do so. It is overly US-centric in both tenor and tone. US policy must address the reality of China's power, influence and appeal. It will continue to increase and slowly supplant the US as the sole leader and arbiter of "the international order." The US must accept this and try to influence the inevitable transition by negotiating the manner, pace and substance of power sharing.

News Flash

Harada (2019), reporting on the opening session of the March 2019 National People's Congress, noted:

Chinese Premier Li Keqiang was conspicuously silent on the "Made in China 2025" initiative as he spoke at the opening session of the National People's Congress…in a likely acknowledgment of harsh U.S. criticism against Beijing's pet industry-building program. This is the first time Li stayed silent on the program in his annual report to the congress since 2015, when he first introduced it…. Other top officials and state news media have already been shying away from the topic for some time…. It is one of the key sticking points in China's trade talks with the U.S. But the shedding of the 2025 plan could be in name only. In his 100-minute-plus speech, Li touched on many aspects of Made in China 2025, including pledging to invest heavily in emerging industries…. The US-China trade war continues and so does its influence on Chinese policy. "Made in China 2025" has been a major campaign of Xi's OBOR/BRI since 2015. The times are, however, apparently changing.

REFERENCES

 Bloomberg News, 2018b. "How 'Made in China 2025' Frames Trump's Trade Threats." *Bloomberg* (April 10).

 Bloomberg News, 2018c. "US Accuses Chinese Spies of Campaign to Steal Jet Engine Tech." *Bloomberg* (October 31).

 Bloomberg Quint, 2018. "Trump Is Targeting China's Push to Make Its Economy High-Tech" *Bloomberg Quint* (March 28).

 CNBC, 2018. "Facing US blowback, Beijing softens its 'Made in China 2025' message." *CNBC Asia-Pacific News* (June 25).

 Cyrill, M., 2018. "What is Made in China 2025 and Why Has it Made the World So Nervous?" *China Briefing* (December 28).

 Harada, I., 2019. "Beijing drops 'Made in China 2025' from government report: Li Keqiang toes around controversial program in nod to US." *Nikkei Asian Review* (March 6).

 HKTDC, 2019. "Made in China Moves to Indonesia," Hong Kong Trade Development Council (January 16).

 Jaipragas, B., 2018. "Trump Strikes a Blow in US-China Struggle with Build Act to Contain Xi's Belt and Road." *South China Morning Post* (October 20).

 Klein, J.X. and R. Delaney, 2019. "US Senator Marco Rubio proposes legislation to counter 'Made in China 2025' while top China hands warn White House to 'course correct' Beijing relationship." *South China Morning Post* (February 12).

 McBride, J., 2018. "Is 'Made in China 2025' a Threat to Global Trade?" Council on Foreign Relations (August 2).

 Saldinger, A., 2018. "How BUILD Act came to be." Devex (December 5).

 Thrush, G., 2018. "Trump Embraces Foreign Aid to Counter China's Global Influence." *New York Times* (October 14).

 Trivedi, A., 2018. "China's Made in 2025 Plan is a Paper Tiger." *Bloomberg Opinion* (December 15).

U.S. Chamber of Commerce, 2017. *Made in China 2025: Global Ambitions Built on Local Protections*. Washington, D.C. (March).

 Valencia, M.J., 2019. "A US strategy that seeks to 'manage' China based only on American interests may be a fool's errand." *South China Morning Post* (February 12).

 Wübbeke, J., M. Meissner, M.J. Zenglein, J. Ives and B. Conrad, 2016. "Made in China 2025: The making of a high-tech superpower and consequences for industrial countries." MERICS Papers on China [Mercator Institute for China Studies] #2 (December).

Michael H. Glantz

PART II

Concepts of OBOR/BRI

Bilateral Tendencies vs. Multilateralism

China's traditional go-it-alone (bilateral) policy can be witnessed by its involvement in the Cold War era's Group of Non-aligned Nations, of which there were 77. The Group became the Group of 77+1, with the +1 being China. China's go-it-alone tendency recently reappeared in similar fashion. In the early days of OBOR in which China worked with 16 central, eastern and southeastern European countries, they created the "Group of 16+1" and, once again, the +1 was China.

Late in 2013, following the launch of OBOR, China began the process of creating a multilateral development bank, the AIIB, which began operating in January 2016 and has since engaged in providing development loans and investments. By the end of 2017, "AIIB's approved membership has risen from 57 to 84, expanding our reach within Asia and around the world," noted the Bank's Vice President. (Wang Jun, 2018) By the end of 2018 its membership had grown to 93. As AIIB's largest shareholder, China has the dominant decision-making power, which is supposed to diminish but not be relinquished as additional members contribute to the Bank.

As OBOR/BRI has expanded well beyond expectations, so too has the influence of the AIIB. China's World-Bank-like AIIB sent a message to Western development banks that China was embarking on a major step-like change in its "going out" involvement in the world of international development assistance. Its official website (AIIB, 2018) noted that:

We are…a multilateral development bank with a mission to improve social and economic outcomes in Asia and beyond. Headquartered in Beijing…. By investing in sustainable infrastructure and other productive sectors today, we will better connect people, services and markets that over time will

Fig. 15 This political cartoon suggests that China is tightening its belt around the globe. *D. Reljic, BOLD.*

impact the lives of billions and build a better future.

On the third anniversary of AIIB its President, Jin Liqun, responded in an interview to a question on its creation. (Yu and Wang, 2019) He noted that "The AIIB is the result of four decades of reform and opening-up of China (e.g., 1978). Without this economic growth, there would be no way that China could take the initiative to establish the bank. With the experiences obtained during those four decades, China can offer valuable insight into promoting infrastructure and other production-related projects through the AIIB." Later in the interview, Jin stated that "the significance of the AIIB is not just to provide additional funding to the gap in infrastructure building, but to diversify the means of international economic and financial cooperation."

At present, it has partnered with the World Bank, the Asian Development Bank and the European Bank of Reconstruction and Development to fund infrastructure projects. China claims that AIIB is devoid of corruption and of political influence. It also claims that, unlike other Western multilateral development institutions, it does not have a veto power, even though it is AIIB's creator and benefactor. On this point, Wang Lei (2018) wrote:

China's position in the AIIB is essentially different from that of other major countries in some other multilateral lenders. For instance, it is different from the veto rights of the US in the IMF or the World Bank and the dominance enjoyed by the US and Japan in the Asian Development Bank. China's high share in the AIIB and its high voting power is temporary. Quotas will be adjusted with more members' participation, *but it is not necessary for China to give up its role.* (italics added)

According to a research fellow at a university-based Chinese finance institute, "AIIB aims to establish itself as a new type of international multilateral development bank in the 21st Century through its sound framework of governance and innovation operation model." (quoted in Wang Jun, 2018)

Bank president Jin commented that "AIIB concentrates [its efforts] in the field of infrastructure building and other production-related fields."

In an article entitled "China's Creditor Imperialism," Chellaney (2017) noted some differences between western loans and Chinese loans:

Unlike International Monetary Fund and World Bank lending, Chinese loans are collateralized by strategically important natural assets with high long-term value (even if they lack short-term commercial viability). [Sri Lanka's Chinese-constructed deep-water port of] Hambantota, for example, straddles Indian Ocean trade routes linking Europe, Africa, and the Middle East to Asia. In exchange for financing and building the infrastructure that poorer countries need, China demands favorable access to their natural assets, from mineral resources to ports…. Rather than offering grants or concessionary loans, China provides huge project-related loans at market-based rates without transparency, much less environmental- or social-impact assessments.

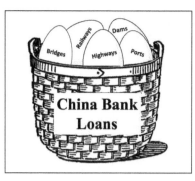

Fig. 16 There is a saying that warns about putting all your eggs in one basket. Should countries be relying on only Chinese banks for their infrastructure loans and construction? *CCB. Adapted from Xia Qing/GT.*

While the AIIB seems to get the most media attention with regard to financial support for OBOR/BRI projects, there are several Chinese banks involved in providing support for various initiative-related projects. These include, among others, the Silk Road Fund, the Export-Import Bank of China, the China Development Bank (CDB), the Industrial and Commercial Bank of China (ICBC), the Bank of China (BOC) and the China Construction Bank (CCB). In addition, other international development banks such as the World Bank have been providing some support for OBOR-related projects. The IMF has also become involved in the initiative as a result of requests from OBOR/BRI partner countries for financial support to help meet their Chinese loan obligations. Some China banks have created branches in the partnering countries.

The risks of loan terms have become clearer over the first five years of OBOR to both the lenders and the borrowers. Now lenders are taking more interest in a partnering country's ability to meet its loan obligations. For their part, borrowing partners now realize that some participating countries in the initiative have fallen unwittingly into a debt trap that has already led to some form or level of a Chinese takeover of the infrastructure development projects, in terms of either ownership or long-term management, e.g., the Hambantota port. In fact, Chinese agreements with Pakistan, Myanmar and Malaysia serve as examples of loan agreements being revised and loan amounts being reduced.

REFERENCES

 AIIB, 2018. "AIIB Granted Permanent Observer Status by the United Nations." AIIB (December 21).

 Chellaney, B., 2017. "China's Creditor Imperialism." *Project Syndicate* (December 20).

 Wang, Jun., 2018. "AIIB Two Years On." *Beijing Review* (February 1) p. 32.

 Wang, Lei. 2018. "AIIB gives China experience in multilateral leadership." *Global Times* (April 22).

Yu, L. and E. Wang, 2019. "Banking on Cooperation: AIIB President Jin Liqun reviews the performance of the China-led multilateral development bank in its first three years." *News China*, Vol. No. 127 (March). pp. 13-15.

OBOR's Belts and Roads as Spheres of Influence

Sphere of Influence is an age-old power-laden concept, the existence of which has been proven through reviews of historical relationships and activities among political units, from tribes to states to regional organizations. It became most explicit in agreements during the colonial partitioning of Africa at the Congress of Berlin in 1884-85. For example, colonial rulers such as Great Britain, France, Belgium, Italy, Portugal, Spain and Germany identified regions in Africa over which each would have sole dominant sovereign interest. One hundred years ago American Political Scientist Quincy Wright (1918) referred to geographical "Spheres of Influence" (SOI) as determined by "territorial propinquity." Wright wrote that:

In its recognition of territorial propinquity... inspection of the cases shows that they may be classified according as geographic proximity has been mentioned to justify (1) the annexation of territory, (2) the enjoyment of special economic privileges, (3) the exercise of extra-territorial jurisdiction, or (4) the protection of special political interests. Territorial, economic, jurisdictional, and political interests have each been presented on occasion as deserving special consideration in neighboring territory.

At the time of his writings, Wright's key phrase, "neighboring territory," had to be an integral aspect of a sphere of influence relationship, whereby one party to the relationship would be in an inferior position (unequal in some way) to a dominant party. For example, in 1823 US President James Monroe issued a statement (that later became known as the Monroe Doctrine), unilaterally declaring that the Western Hemisphere was off limits to military or other interventions from European countries, while in essence reserving its own right to intervene in countries throughout the hemisphere. Monroe's statement made no mention of interference from Asian countries.

As Asian and African nations emerged from colonialism after WWI and WWII, the Soviet Union, which had helped to liberate Eastern European countries from Nazi domination, chose to keep control over the liberated region within its geographic SOI, placing it under its ideological SOI as well. Eastern Europe became a Soviet buffer to the influences of Western capitalism and any resurgence of military threat to the USSR from the West. With the breakup of the Soviet Union in 1991, its loss of control over Eastern Europe sparked the desire by the various liberated countries to join NATO and the European Union.

Another interesting example of the SOI concept is Cuba. While Cuba is in the geographic SOI of the United States as a result of territorial propinquity, i.e., 90 miles offshore of the US State of Florida, it has been within the Soviet ideological and economic SOI since 1960. Cuba's relationship with the USSR was as a Soviet Union functional SOI, based on their common ideological interests but not on territorial propinquity.

The *Wikipedia* (2018) definition of an SOI in the field of international relations comes closest to the distinction we want to make between geographic and functional SOIs with regard to China's OBOR. An SOI:

...is a spatial region or concept division over which a state or organization has a level of cultural, economic, military, or political exclusivity, accommodating to the interests of powers outside the borders of the state that controls it.

While there may be a formal alliance or other treaty obligations between the influenced and influencer, such formal arrangements are not necessary and the influence can often be more of an example of soft power [the power of persuasion as opposed to the power of force]. Similarly, a formal alliance does not necessarily mean that one country lies within another's sphere of influence.... In more extreme cases, a country within the "sphere

Michael H. Glantz

of influence" of another may become a subsidiary of that state and serve in effect as a satellite state or *de facto* colony. The system of spheres of influence by which powerful nations intervene in the affairs of others continues to the present.

We argue that OBOR/BRI basically started out as a traditional interpretation of a geographic sphere-of-influence concept relating to infrastructure projects on land and sea, tracking a modern-day, idealized, land-based, ancient Silk Road from China in the Far East to Western Europe, the Middle East and Northeastern Africa. The positive responses from developing economies encouraged China to identify functional silk belts and roads. There is always a functional aspect to a geographic "silk road," although the primary purpose for its creation can be either "place or activity" based. While the original six belts and roads plus the Polar Silk Road are basically based on "place," China has since identified new silk roads based primarily on function, such as a digital silk road and a space silk road. These can be classified as China's functional spheres of influence.

In an article about Vietnam's prolonged and mixed responses to OBOR/BRI, Hiep (2018) introduced another way to talk about China's expansive view of its SOI: "BRI's geographical scope." This new framing of the OBOR/BRI Initiative could be used to shift discussion about the underlying reasons for the Initiative to motivations based on a humanitarian *connectivity perspective* rather than based on a political *country-specific (e.g., China) perspective* as being the less political, less hegemonic driving force behind it.

REFERENCES

 Hiep, L. H., 2018. "The Belt and Road Initiative in Vietnam: Challenges and Prospects." ISEAS – Yusof Ishak Institute (Singapore), p. 2. (March 29).

 Wikipedia, 2018. "Spheres of Influence" (September 2).

 Wright, Q., 1918. "Territorial Propinquity." *The American Journal of International Law*. Vol. 12, No. 3 (July, 1918), pp. 519-561.

Geographic and Functional Silk Roads as "Campaigns"

Faster and more voluminous trade with Europe and countries along the way, by land (the belt) and by sea (the road), would be economically advantageous for all countries and companies involved in the Initiative.

China focused on constructing or rehabilitating decaying infrastructure domestically and abroad: infrastructure encompasses roads, railways, ports, oil pipelines, airports, dams, energy grids and the like, within the country as well as internationally. By self-admission, its assistance was not designed to be humanitarian foreign aid. It was loan-based financing for those developing countries participating in the OBOR/BRI network that were sorely in need of improved infrastructure in order to enhance their national and regional economic development prospects. One could say that "place" was the first concern in developing what, in essence, would be a geographically-based sphere of influence over the long term: Europe, Central Asia, Middle East, Southeast Asia, Europe and Northeastern Africa. The geographic set of belts and roads was expanded with the inclusion of new spheres of influence in the polar region and in the Western Hemisphere.

The successes of OBOR/BRI have encouraged China to continue to identify new roads. Those newer "roads," however, are not primarily based on specific geographic considerations. They are "functional" silk roads (e.g., functional SOIs) that include such activities as cyber, digital, and space. With functional roads or belts, the function (what gets done) is of primary concern and place (where what gets done gets done) is secondary. A digital silk road network, for example, links OBOR/BRI countries together in a network that China can manage and, if it so chooses, can dominate without having to answer to Western digital powers or institutions.

There are now additional functional silk roads inside

Fig. 17 "Spread positive energy and build the China Dream," propaganda poster under the leadership of Xi. *Tupian114, China Dream.*

China that are focused on security, health and safety, among others likely to be created. The new officially designated functional roads, e.g., functional spheres of influence, suggest that perhaps such roads are China's 21st Century way of generating and organizing internal support for government-inspired initiatives that are not directly or exclusively related to infrastructure. In other words, Belts and Roads are China's 21st Century "campaigns."

Starting in the 1930s, the Communist Party under Chairman Mao developed campaigns designed to inspire (and later force) people to engage in certain Party-approved socio-economic, political, and cultural activities. Several articles have been written about the use of slogans by Chinese leaders to motivate, educate, inform or instruct the general population on what the Communist regime expects of it: what the people need to learn; what they must know; and, perhaps most important of all, how to behave. Kelkar (1978) observed that "the political campaign usually involved recognition of the problem, indication of the seriousness of the problem, selection of desired goals and arriving at decisions as to the appropriate line of action that might be taken."

Though slogans were used before the Chinese Communist regime came to power in 1949, the Communist regime raised "sloganeering" to a new level for a variety of reasons: ideological and political correctness, enhancing productivity, attacking corruption, targeting anti-regime thinking and "encouraging" voluntary activities, e.g., sending students to collective farms to work with their hands.

Many articles have noted that such slogans have transformed China: "Let 100 Flowers Bloom" (1956); "Dare to think, dare to act" (1958); "Going up to the Mountains, Down to the Countryside" (1968); "Smash the Gang of Four" (1976); "Reform and opening up" (1978); "Have fewer children, raise more pigs" (1979); "Achieve the four modernizations" (1978). Slogans such as these appeared frequently during the formative early decades of the Peoples Republic of China. One observer suggested that "Mao elevated political sloganeering to an art form." (Boyle, 2013)

Fast forward to the first decades of the 21st Century. An article entitled "Xi Jinping carries on China's hallowed tradition of political slogans dating back to Mao" (*Associated Press News*, 2015) noted that "Political slogans have been a mainstay of Chinese life dating back to Mao Zedong, founder of the People's Republic…. President Xi Jinping is carrying on that tradition with two of his slogans, 'Chinese Dream of the Great Rejuvenation of the Chinese Nation' and the 'Four Comprehensives.'"

China continues to use slogans to launch social, economic and political campaigns to mobilize its people. Xi's OBOR/BRI Initiative is, therefore, in line with Chinese leadership's historical use of slogans. His initiative began with six "pathways;" within five years several new roads have been developed (e.g., polar, digital, space, cyber,

security). Each new road is in fact a campaign designed to motivate, mobilize, inspire people, companies, government ministries and agencies as well as provincial governments. The initial slogan, "One Belt One Road," has proven to be a treasure trove for President Xi and for his "One Dream" slogan.

However, Ang (2018) noted that "China has never expanded one of its campaigns overseas before and wasn't prepared for the bureaucratic challenges it would face. Similarly, its international partners are for the most part novices at dealing with Chinese companies and banks. The result has been mass confusion with hits and misses."

Ang's article, "Needed for China's Belt and Road: A Road Map" questions the future of OBOR/BRI, suggesting that "right now, like most Communist Party campaigns, it's sprawling and uncoordinated." Ang's opening sentences set the stage for his concern: "Strategists in the West fear that China's Belt and Road Initiative is a vast, well-laid and finely orchestrated plan to extend Chinese hegemony over much of the developing world. They should be afraid of something else: It's nothing of the sort…. While outsiders tend to credit Chinese leaders with long-term vision and exquisite strategizing, policy implementation has in fact often been fragmented and patchy." Ang concluded with "The Belt and Road isn't a master plan: It needs one."

REFERENCES

 Ang, Y.Y., 2018. "China's Belt and Road Is a Capaign, Not a Conspiracy." *Bloomberg* (September 27).

 Associated Press News, 2015. "Xi Jinping carries on China's hallowed tradition of political slogans dating back to Mao." *Fox News* (March 6).

 Boyle, J., 2013. "11 slogans that changed China." *BBC News* (December 26).

Kelkar, G.S., 1978. "The Chinese Experience of Political Campaigns and Mass Mobilization." *Social Scientist*, Vol. 7, #5 (December), pp. 45-63.

PART III

The Great Games

Let the Great Games Begin

The Great Game was the name given to the strategic rivalry between the British Empire and the Russian Empire for supremacy in central Asia during the 19th century. (Samandi, 2017) The two empires sought control over the territory between the Russian Empire to its south and British Empire's dominance over India. The British wanted a buffer in central and southwestern Asia between its Indian possession and an expanding Tsarist Russia. Their rivalry continued in the region from the 1830s to 1907, when an agreement was reached by the two empires at the expense of the independence or the territorial integrity of the countries and khanates in-between.

With respect to OBOR/BRI, we view the "Great Game" concept as a "social invention," that is, a concept that can attract attention to a situation and can influence political behavior of governments worldwide. The Great Game is used to highlight the regional and global significance of China's 2013 launching of the "One Belt One Road" Initiative. President Xi's "going out" policy (e.g., going outside its international borders) to "Make China a Global Power Again" comes at a time when power conflicts have been heating up on various continents: US vs. China, Russia vs. China, US vs. Russia, India vs. China, Saudi Arabia vs. Iran, China vs. EU, US vs. China in Latin America, US favors India, China favors Pakistan, etc.

These new great games are emerging at a time when US policies have turned to isolationism as its guiding international policy sparked by President Trump's key campaign slogans: "Make America Great Again" and "America First." Trump's political attack on NATO allies as well as on his North American neighbors, while praising authoritarian leaders (e.g., Russia's Putin, the Philippines

Fig. 18 The Great Game in Central Asia: Origin of the great game concept. *Woodrow Wilson Center Press.*

Duterte and North Korea's Kim), provided political space worldwide for China to elevate its stature as a global political force to be reckoned with.

In the sections that follow, we look at China's interactions through its OBOR/BRI as continental and regional Great Games in the short to midterm with long-term consequences for governance on the planet. A US-dominated, Western-based political and economic system has prevailed since the end of World War II. That system today is being challenged by the People's Republic of China through President Xi's pursuit of China's decades-old "going out" policy on proverbial steroids, announcing that at least $4 trillion in USD equivalent would be used to pull developing countries out of poverty in the short term. China has the credentials to make such a claim as the largest developing country economy, having done so for itself in a few decades. The PRC offers itself as an alternative economic development model to what the West has offered for the past 70 years. China has clearly inspired countries in Asia, Africa and Latin America to give consideration to the Chinese methods that put it on the path to becoming a global superpower.

The Great Game on each continent – and in each country that has chosen to partner with China in Xi's Initiative – is multifaceted and complicated. Each country's story of its development goals, prospects and interactions with the PRC to achieve them is worthy of a lengthy book. Here, we point out some key highlights for the continent and for the specific country examples that are cited. The highlights are tips of an iceberg poking through the ocean surface, while most of the iceberg remains hidden. We have provided numerous references, so the readers can pursue issues or controversies that capture their interest.

Everything with respect to OBOR/BRI seems to be surrounded by controversy. Searching the Internet for an aspect of a country's involvement in OBOR (and later BRI) yields for the most part pro and con comments from supporters and detractors, respectively. It is like watching a complex mystery video halfway and the outcome of the plot has not yet become clear, given its twists and turns. That is similar to watching the news about OBOR/BRI projects in the news weekly if not daily. We relied on public sources of information. We were not privy to the secret political or ideological deliberations of governments involved. This is especially true for the PRC. We do find insights, eventually, from investigative reporting of the free press into other countries' decision-making processes due to the adage "ships of state tend to leak from the top."

Each Great Game we mention raises a myriad of issues, some resolved, some ongoing and some with yet to be determined outcomes. In this primer we have selected a few issues to note with the hope, if not expectation, of capturing the reader's interest in an aspect or the totality of any or all of the games identified herein. There are likely to be Great Game features we have missed. Our primer is meant to be a spark to generate interest in international politics at the superpower level at a time when the US is relinquishing its global superpower status and renouncing its *de facto* role as the planet's policeman, while the PRC is seemingly striving for both of those global roles. Is the creation of a China-centric world possible, as a result of OBOR's grand vision of connecting most of the world around China? (Wu *et al.*, 2017)

REFERENCES

 Samandi, I., 2017. "What was 'the Great Game'?" *Quora* (October 28).

 Wu, Y., C. Alden, and E. Sidiropoulos, 2017. "Where Africa fits into China's massive Belt and Road Initiative." *The Conversation* (May).

India, Pakistan, and China

India and China have a history of conflict that serves as the backdrop for their present-day interactions related to the Belt and Road Initiative. Ever since One Belt One Road was launched in 2013, India has viewed and treated the initiative as suspect. It did not trust the political motives behind China's "going out" policy. India's neighbors on land and sea, however, at first saw Chinese development loans as providing a pathway to national economic development. One by one, each embraced OBOR/BRI, agreeing to take loans that eventually could strain their national budgets.

Over the course of the past five years, under Xi's OBOR/BRI, China's (various governments and state-owned enterprises) have negotiated their involvement with over 70 countries and organizations in Africa, Asia, the Middle East, Latin America, and Europe. From India's perspective, most importantly, several of those OBOR-partnering countries were encircling them. Along with Chinese loans for infrastructure development throughout the region, China's investments in Pakistan have been especially worrisome to India, as China was strengthening its influence in Pakistan. The *fait accompli* for India, however, was that China had agreed with Pakistan to have its infrastructure development projects cut across what India considers its territory, the part of India's State of Kashmir occupied by Pakistan. This was taking place at a time when US policies toward Pakistan were turning against that country.

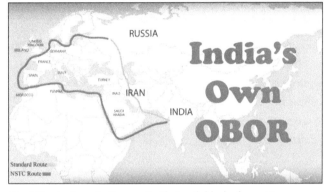

Fig. 19 India seeks its own North-South block of countries as an alternative to China's OBOR. *Global Conflict.*

Fig. 20 Pakistan is a key partner for China's Belt and Road Initiative. It is a red-flag relationship to India, Pakistan's regional rival. *PakObserver.*

China, its regional rival, had encroached – through OBOR/BRI – on what India considered to be its geographic sphere of influence based on territorial propinquity. China had made infrastructure loan arrangements with Afghanistan, Pakistan, Myanmar, The Maldives, Sri Lanka, and Nepal, and had been completing its encirclement of India with OBOR/BRI discussions with Bangladesh. The encirclement was not only land-based. Several of China's infrastructure projects were undertaken to gain access to the Indian Ocean and its rim countries through loans for the development of railways, and oil and gas pipelines, and deep-water ports such as Pakistan's port of Gwadar and Myanmar's port of Kyaukpyu. The deep-water port with a special economic zone in Djibouti provided China with a military base at a strategic location on the western edge of the Indian Ocean.

The idea of a new Silk Road program had actually been considered by the United States in 2011, as a political response to China's pre-OBOR bilateral activities in Central Asia. At that time, the US sought to promote India-led integration through North-South silk road trade and economy that would include Afghanistan, Southwestern and Central Asia states, Pakistan, and India. It was later described by the U.S. State Department (2015) "as a complement to the [OBOR] East-West connection across Eurasia."

In fact, India's North-South Transportation Corridor (NSTC) Project involving Afghanistan, Russia, Iran and Pakistan was a response to China's strategic regional focus and funding of $60 billion USD for more than 60 projects in Pakistan through CPEC (China Pakistan Economic Corridor). China has actively been solidifying its relationship on various dimensions with Pakistan. The new roads, railways and pipelines and the deep-water port at Gwadar are of great strategic significance to China. The Gwadar port provides western China's landlocked Xinjiang Uighur Autonomous Region with a shortcut to the Indian Ocean for its exports. The pipeline from Gwadar is also important for transporting Mideast oil to China. (ANI, 2018)

India has been highly critical of China's growing influence in Pakistan, and especially angered that key Chinese-Pakistan projects under CPEC pass through the Pakistan-occupied portion of Kashmir. The bottom line is that India, worried and suspicious of China's motives, considers the OBOR/BRI as a proverbial Trojan Horse gift from China to neighboring countries, as suggested in the following political cartoon.

Despite India's "on again, off again" attacks on China's OBOR/BRI, it continues to be a major trading partner with China. Most recently, India proposed a new plan that complements China's plans on the Indian sub-continent. Bhaya (2018) reported on a positive shift in India's policy toward OBOR/BRI. "India has offered China connectivity through its northeastern region to Bangladesh's Chittagong port on the Indian Ocean as part of an ambitious multilateral plan that appears to complement the Bangladesh, China, India, Myanmar (BCIM) Economic Corridor proposed under Beijing's…BRI." It appears that India is more open to engage China in multilateral projects rather than in bilateral arrangements as China has done with her neighbors.

Baluchi Opposition to China's Activities in Pakistan

India is not alone in its distrust of China's interactions in Pakistan. There are Pakistani concerns as well about those Chinese development infrastructure-related projects. Perhaps an extreme example of such discontent can be found in the country's largest province, Baluchistan. Kuhn (2010) entitled his article about Pakistan with a title that has foreshadowed today's reality in Pakistan: "Modern-day 'Great Game' Plays Out in Baluchistan."

Huang (2018) wrote that "Baluchistan is at the heart of [CPEC] and is home to the port of Gwadar, where Beijing is said to be developing its second overseas military base." "The Chinese have helped to build and run the port of Gwadar." (Kuhn, 2010) This port is of great importance to China's land-locked western regions, especially Xinjiang. CPEC's infrastructure projects of railways, highways and pipeline links provide an outlet to the Arabian Sea and a shortcut to Middle East oil.

The problem for both Pakistan and for China is that Baluchistan's majority Baluch ethnic population has been a restive province politically, since the creation of Pakistan as a nation. Kuhn (2010) noted that "Almost since Pakistan's birth, its government has been battling a low-level insurgency in the southwest region of Baluchistan."

He also noted that "The Baluch are deeply divided between seeking outright independence for Baluchistan and seeking autonomy within Pakistan." In any event Baluchs are concerned about the increasing Chinese influence in their Province and the potential weakening of their cultural identity, as a result of OBOR/BRI projects and the Chinese workers that are brought in to construct them. (e.g., Kynge, 2018a)

There is, in fact, a Baloch Revolutionary Army

Fig. 21 China's trojan horse gift to Pakistan is CPEC, according to India. *C. Crowe, Times of India.*

Michael H. Glantz

that has in the past attacked the Pakistani government and carried out deadly attacks on Chinese workers. (Notezai, 2018) Huang's following headline exposes a major underlying threat to OBOR/BRI projects not only in Baluchistan but in other countries as well: "Pakistan attacks expose China's Achilles' heel on international stage."

For Pakistan to protect the construction and operation of their infrastructure projects, Huang reported "The Pakistani government has promised to deploy 10,000 soldiers to protect a port development that forms part of the CPEC." China has been considering a range of ways – from using PLA troops to private Chinese security companies – to enhance its security needs abroad for its OBOR/BRI projects and its Chinese workers on such projects. This has been a growing general concern for its international infrastructure projects in partner countries. (Wuthnow, 2018)

Kuhn captured an interesting Baluchi observation:

Baluch nationalist and former senator Tahir Bizenjo hears in all of this [the] historical echoes of the days when the British and Russian empires once fought proxy wars and vied for spheres of influence in Baluchistan. "To me, the 19th-century 'Great Game' has started in this region again…but in different forms and with different players."

Pakistan's CPEC: Debt Trap or Military Diplomacy or Both?

One could argue that Pakistan's $60+ billion in loans for CPEC projects was undertaken with Pakistan's leaders' open eyes as well as open hands. Aside from a lack of transparency, and corruption at the highest levels of the Pakistan Government, these two countries share a common border and share a concern about common political enemies (e.g., India and the US). In addition, Pakistani factories are building Chinese military equipment including aircraft.

The port of Gwadar provides China access to the Arabian Sea from its Muslim-dominated western landlocked Xinjiang. Like other deep-water ports that Chinese engineers and workers have been constructing, civilian ports and their accompanying economic zones can also be used for military purposes. Abi-Habib (2018) commented on the port of Gwadar, noting that "it also gives Beijing a strategic card to play against India and the United States if tensions worsen to the point of naval blockades as the two powers increasingly confront each other at sea."

China's overseas port system in the Indian Ocean is called its "string of pearls." Close scrutiny of those maritime pearls, the ports and their accompanying free trade zones, shows how China has been expanding its military as well as its commercial influence around the Indian Ocean. Abi-Habib reported that "Chinese officials have repeatedly said the Belt and Road is purely an economic project with peaceful intent. But with its plan for Pakistan, China is for the first time explicitly tying the Belt and Road proposal to its military ambitions.... Even before the revelation of the new Chinese-Pakistani cooperation, some of China's biggest projects in Pakistan had clear strategic implications." (see also Toppa, 2018) CPEC is Pakistan's military project with clearly little involvement of civilian governments, and both China and Pakistan are pursuing military agendas with a common goal to contain India in Afghanistan and in the region, and the US as well. China is already playing an active role in Afghanistan as well and wants it to be part of CPEC economic and strategic interests to connect with Central Asia. China's role in Afghanistan is mainly via Pakistan and moving toward, and now working directly with, the Afghan government, which in the future may be of concern to Pakistan.

The Maldives: Second Thoughts on OBOR/BRI

A most recent move by India has been to help neighboring Maldives combat a likely OBOR/BRI debt trap. The Maldives cannot repay its $3 billion USD debt to China to construct infrastructure that had been negotiated and agreed-to by the current president's predecessor. Marlow and Li (2018) reported a recent government official comment on its loans from China: "'We have been burned,' said Economic Development Minister Fayzal Ismail. The tourist paradise of the Maldives isn't the only Asian nation to discover that the promise of Chinese President Xi Jinping's signature program is too good to be true."

India's Prime Minister Modi came to the rescue by offering a $1.4 billion line of credit to the Maldives government to help keep that government solvent. More importantly to India, the credit would strengthen India's relationship with the Maldives while weakening that country's ties to China. Kuronuma (2018) observed that "India, alarmed by China's growing influence in the Indian Ocean region, appears eager to bring the Maldives back under its wing by helping the new government repay the Chinese." Kuronuma also mentioned the likely influence of Sri Lanka's debt trap on India's decision to intervene in the Maldives debt-to-China problem: "Sri Lanka, another one of India's neighbors, has given up control of a port in the southern district of Hambantota to the Chinese in exchange for debt relief. India is anxious to prevent a similar development in the Maldives." The support for Maldives disrupts encirclement of India by China's OBOR/BRI country partners.

REFERENCES

 ANI, 2018. "China's BRI initiative hits roadblock in 7 countries: report." *The Economic Times* (April 15).

 Abi-Habib, M., 2018. "China's 'Belt and Road' plan in Pakistan takes a military turn." *New York Times* (Dec, 19).

 Bhaya, A., 2018. "India offers China access to northeast in BRI strategic shift." *CGTN* (August 30).

 Huang, K., 2018. "Pakistan attacks expose China's Achilles' heel on international stage." *South China Morning Post* (December 3).

 Kuhn, A., 2010. "Modern-Day 'Great Game' Plays Out in Baluchistan." *NPR (National Public Radio)* transcript. October 15.

 Kuronuma, Y., 2018. "India offers Maldives $1.4bn package amid China debt worries." *Nikkei Asian Review* (December 18).

 Kynge, J., 2018a. "Chinese contractors grab lion's share of Silk Road projects" *Financial Times* (January 24).

 Marlow, I. and D. Li, 2018. "How Asia Fell Out of Love with China's Belt and Road Initiative." Bloomberg (December 10).

 Notezai, M.A., 2018. "Why Balochs Are Targeting China" *The Diplomat* (November 26).

 Toppa, S., 2018. "Why Young Pakistanis Are Learning Chinese." Th Atlantic (November 14).

 U.S. State Department, 2015. "U.S. Support for the New Silk Road." (March 6).

 Wuthnow, J., 2018. "Securing China's Belt and Road Initiative: Dimensions and Implications." Testimony before the U.S.-China Economic and Security Review Commission Hearing on "China's Belt and Road Initiative: Five Years Later." USCC (January 25).

Iran, China, and OBOR/BRI

Iran is in the midst of many political, ideological and economic controversies – globally, regionally and nationally. It is being pulled and pushed in various directions, and not each direction is complementary to the others. Here, we mention three interesting aspects of Iran's relationship with China with regard to the OBOR/BRI: (1) the US withdrawal from the Iran nuclear non-proliferation agreement with Iran; (2) the apparent strength of the relationship between China and Iran; and, (3) the set of OBOR activities that China has been undertaking in Iran.

(1) US withdrawal from the Iran nuclear non-proliferation agreement with Iran

The US under Trump has withdrawn from an agreement that the Obama Administration had signed with Iran and other countries (France, Germany, UK, Russia, European Union, China) in mid-2015. The JCPOA (Joint Comprehensive Plan of Action) was to ensure that Iran's nuclear program would be exclusively for peaceful purposes. The agreement had led to a suspension of US economic sanctions against Iran and any country that trades with it. When the US decided to withdraw from the Iran nuclear deal, it opened up the certainty that US sanctions would be re-imposed.

Aside from the problems created for Iran's economy, problems would also be created for countries and business entities with which it has interactions. As an *OBOReurope* (2018a) article suggested, "US withdrawal from this agreement may have several consequences on relations between China and Iran and the development of the new Silk Roads." The article also suggested that the US withdrawal could strengthen the internationalization of the Chinese currency, RMB. In fact, "Since 2012, Iran has accepted Chinese currency for its crude oil exports to Beijing…. To avoid US sanctions, the euro and the RMB could be used jointly by other states in their relations with Iran."

(2) The apparent strength of the relationship between China and Iran

For about a decade, China and Iran have been important trading partners, as China seeks oil, gas and mineral resources to fuel its economy. Since then, their relationship for economic interactions has intensified, reinforced by regional political issues: along with Russia, they both support Syria's Assad regime. For its part, President Xi's China is pursuing a "going out" policy more aggressively. To that end, developing the new economic silk roads must involve Iran, given its central crossroad location between China and Europe. In addition, by befriending Iran, a Muslim country, it creates a Muslim ally to the west of China's Muslim-dominated Xinjiang. Partnering with Iran through OBOR, cements their political, cultural, economic, and military relationships. In addition to Iran being a major exporter of crude oil to China, Erdbrink (2017) observed that "Chinese state companies are active all over the country, building highways, digging mines and making steel. Tehran's shops are flooded with Chinese products and its streets clogged with Chinese cars."

A Pakistani colleague noted (private communication, January 19, 2019): "Iran is providing access to China with major contracts in Syria and Iraq and strengthening its strategic relationship through creating business opportunities in return for China's active partnership in the Iran nuclear deal," from which the US under president Trump has withdrawn.

(3) The set of OBOR/BRI activities China has been undertaking in Iran

Erdbrink (2017) noted:

For China's Global Ambitions, "Iran is at the Center of Everything." Geographically, Iran is as central to the success of OBOR as is Kazakhstan. Iran was on the ancient Silk Road and is an integral part of the New Economic Silk Road.

Like pieces of a sprawling geopolitical puzzle, components of China's infrastructure network are being put in place. In Eastern Iran, Chinese workers are busily modernizing one of the country's major rail routes, standardizing gauge sizes, improving the track bed and rebuilding bridges, with the ultimate goal of connecting Tehran to Turkmenistan and Afghanistan. Much of the same is happening in western Iran, where crews are working to link the capital to Turkey and, eventually, Europe. Other rail projects will connect Tehran and Mashhad with deep-water ports in the country's south.

Central Asia, Southwest Asia and the Middle East are embroiled in political rivalries, military conflicts, and proxy wars. Major powers are interested in the region: the US, Russia, India, Pakistan, Iran, and China. This is the setting in which the Chinese are pursuing Belt and Road infrastructure and trade projects. China is not concerned to date with stability or instability in OBOR partner countries it seeks to work with through loan arrangements. This is no doubt in Iran's favor, considering the insecure state of its rail, power, retail and distribution networks. If China is able to establish a secure railway, it will provide more than enough oil to meet its domestic demands. Of course, China is an experienced hand.

A new key silk route traverses Pakistan from north to its southern coast and port of Gwadar. However, the Pakistani economy is weak and the government has become concerned about the rumor of China's so called debt trap.

In need of funds, Pakistan has been courting a financial partnership in regard to OBOR projects with Saudi Arabia, Iran's regional antagonist. Saudi involvement in CPEC projects near Iran's border would likely be unsettling. It is not yet clear what China really thinks about Saudi involvement in OBOR/BRI projects in Pakistan, though Iran has been all too eager to express its displeasure with Saudi Arabia's presence in Pakistan. Foreign Minister Shah Mahmood Quresh was quoted as attributing recent abductions along the Iran-Pakistan border

to "common enemies [who are] unhappy with the existing close friendly relations between Pakistan and Iran," implying Saudi Arabia is responsible. (Aman, 2018) To China, however, Iran is as much an opportunity as a challenge.

Might Saudi Arabia become a new player in the New Eurasian Great Game? The Saudis and Iranians are engaged in a deadly multi-year, seemingly deadlocked, proxy war in Yemen. Dorsey (2017) in his article entitled "The US-Saudi Plot for Iran that spells trouble for China's New Silk Road" suggested that there is a plan to destabilize Iran by supporting the discontent of Iran's Baluchi minority. Such a Saudi plan exists to "foment ethnic unrest" among the Baluchis on the Iranian side of the Iran-Pakistan border. Dorsey observed that:

> US-backed Saudi plans to destabilise Iran threaten to substantially worsen security in the already troubled Pakistan province of Baluchistan.... [Saudi Arabia] sees Iran's ethnic minorities as a way of destabilizing the Islamic republic, if not toppling the government.

Saudi Arabia and the US might believe that such a plan could weaken Iran's resolve to continue a war without end in Yemen.

If such a scenario were to play out, it would create considerable insecurity for OBOR/BRI projects not only in Pakistan (such as the deep-water port of Gwadar) but also in Iran and could even draw India into a conflict. The "fog" of such a new proxy war in Southwest Asia would likely have unfathomable outcomes that could involve China as well. Hopefully, such a scenario is only an errant thought and not a plan.

A Pakistani colleague also noted that China has a big stake in Iran-OBOR connectivity, even more than with Pakistan. Iran already provided road and train access for China to reach Europe and Eurasia. In addition, he noted that Saudi $15 billion USD investment in Gwadar can be viewed as an indirect US plan to counter China's plans of building Gwadar as a dominant strategic advantage. This is why China is pursuing both Iran and Pakistan tracts of BRI in order to offset any negative fallout in future.

REFERENCES

 Aman, F., 2018. "Regional Rivalries Threaten Iran-Pakistan Relations," Atlantic Council. (November 6).

 Dorsey, J.M., 2017. "The US-Saudi Plot for Iran that spells trouble for China's New Silk Road." *South China Morning Post, This Week in Asia* (May 27).

 Erdbrink, T., 2017. "For China's Global Ambitions, 'Iran Is at the Center of Everything'." *New York Times* (July 25).

 OBOReurope, 2018a. "The new Silk Road and Iran." OBOReurope (May 20).

A Great Game in Greater Central Asia

The region historically referred to as Soviet Central Asia includes the 5 Central Asian Republics (CARs) of the Former Soviet Union (FSU): Kazakhstan, Uzbekistan, Turkmenistan, Tajikistan and Kyrgyzstan. Their political status changed drastically when the Soviet Union collapsed in 1991 and they became independent republics. Since the early 1990s, Central Asian leaders have referred on occasion to neighboring Afghanistan as the sixth CAR. In fact, it does occupy 14% of the Aral Sea Basin and its mountains supply about 15% of streamflow to the region's mighty Amu Darya River that used to flow into Central Asia's Aral Sea.

Before the Soviet collapse, the CARs of the USSR were little known to the West, relatively speaking, and had been more or less off limits to foreigners. The region drew considerable environmental interest and elevated international status, because the Aral Sea was rapidly shrinking in the last few decades of the 20th century. The shrinking of the sea was the result of deliberate river diversions from the sea's two major rivers, the Amu Darya and the Syr Darya. The diversions were officially sanctioned by the Soviet Politburo and later by the independent CARs to use river water on fertile but dry desert sands, mainly to grow cotton. The Aral Sea was the fourth-largest inland sea in the world in the 1970s but today it has almost disappeared.

The Central Asian region has now become a political playing field for global as well as regional powers, even though Russia considers its former Central Asia Republics as within its sphere of influence. Regional powers including China, India, Pakistan, Iran and Russia (along with the distant US) are vying for dominant influence in and over the CARs. It is fair to say that all of these countries could be collectively labeled as "Greater Central Asia."

Some of the 5 FSU republics are rich in hydrocarbons (oil, natural gas, coal resources), while others have mineral and water resources. Though they are at various levels of economic development, size, and population, and with different geographic features (desert, mountain, glacial landscapes), they share a common political feature: each republic is landlocked. Idan (2018) stated its significance in the following way:

The major geographic characteristic of the Central Asian countries established following the break-up of the Soviet Union is the fact that they are land-locked. This factor creates challenges in all spheres of development – foreign policy, security, and unique human development.

Idan quoted "Kazakhstan President Nazarbayev [who] stated…that the lack of access to the sea could be detrimental to the country's economic development, and to its political independence, as well as making participation in international economic relations difficult."

As for the sixth CAR, Afghanistan, the prolonged wars in that country have made it difficult to realize major involvement in regional transboundary infrastructure development plans, except for some notable projects with Uzbekistan. (Durso, 2018)

Rehabilitating the existing infrastructure and modernizing it to meet contemporary needs is common and recognized as a necessary key to national development as well as regional cooperation in a Greater Central Asia. Modernization would enhance the regional exchange of goods and services with neighboring as well as foreign markets, including those in China.

China's step-like change in development interest and in expanding its socio-economic and political influence in the region can easily be traced to President Xi's OBOR/ BRI. Each of these countries has received development loans from China through OBOR/BRI. It did so before OBOR/BRI was launched in 2013 and has continued to make such loans today for infrastructure projects such as pipelines for natural gas and oil shipments to China, rail lines and roads for trade interactions, again with China, as well as with other countries. Kazakhstan supplies oil to China, Turkmenistan provides natural gas to China, while others exchange their mineral resources for infrastructure development loans. Furukawa (2018) noted that "Borrowing from Beijing has ballooned in all but… Kazakhstan and Uzbekistan."

Idan (2018) identified some favorable aspects of China's involvement in the region to promote connectivity:

- Connectivity is a factor able to change the geopolitical reality in a region whose geographic location is naturally constant.
- China provided CA states with a regional large-scale plan for connectivity within the region to neighboring countries, but especially to China.
- The BRI integrates the countries of Central Asia with a new and multi-faceted transportation network, as well as connecting Central Asia to faraway countries and markets.
- According to the BRI scheme, Central Asia becomes the main continental gateway for Chinese transportation routes westward.
- Essentially, China is unlocking landlocked Central Asia…. China's BRI can transform Central Asia from its landlocked state to a transit region between Asia and Europe.
- China has provided people-to-people exchanges with the CARs as part of its soft diplomatic efforts to win over popular support and to dissuade local people from their fear of China's potential hegemony.

However, Idan also identified some worrisome aspects of taking Chinese loans. "Central Asian states are well aware of the problematic experiences of some countries with Chinese investments – the Hambantota port in Sri Lanka being the most notable example." Each CAR has knowingly incurred varying levels of debt by the OBOR-related projects.

Comments by Furukawa (2018) highlight concerns about emerging, as well as potential, debt traps for the five CARs. "As Beijing bankrolls projects in Central Asia to promote its Belt and Road Initiative, countries in the region are at risk of granting China valuable concessions to ease their heavy debt burdens." For example, he noted "Tajikistan handed over a gold mine to China in April as remuneration for $300 million in funding to build a power plant" and that "Some predict that Turkmenistan will have to hand over gas fields to China as repayment for its debts."

Cohen (2018) provided advice to Central Asian decision makers:

[W]hile the BRI can be a great facilitator for connectivity and development in the region, Central Asian countries must be active in the management of the belt and road projects passing through their territory if they hope to maximize local input – and impact…. Participants of China's BRI – particularly those which are overly dependent on China as a trade partner or creditor – run the risk of debt spirals and dangerous exposure to markets shocks.

The Kyrgyz Republic and Tajikistan, for example, respectively owe 40% and 50% of their public debt to China.

Cohen and Grant (2018) suggested the following to Central Asian governments seeking Belt and Road loans from China.

Knowing about the debt trap, governments must carefully consider the soft elements of their legal, regulatory, and fiscal infrastructure. How will the projects be structured? What will be the local content and labor requirements to foster the growth of human capital? What are the terms of debt and will the government have future capacity to repay it? Lastly, and perhaps most importantly, are the "rules" and "terms" of each infrastructure project transparent?" (p. 3)

Kairat Moldashev's "Constructive Critique of BRI from Central Asia: A Summary"

Researcher Moldashev (2019) states in his article, "Risks in the Implementation of the 'Belt and Road Initiative' in Central Asia," that "the 'Belt and Road' is a timely initiative for China and other Asian countries." Instead of widely-discussed geopolitical and economic implications of the BRI, his article focused on "other problems that may adversely affect the further development of this initiative: …issues of [1] sustainable development, [2] the absence of control by the PRC over possible corruption schemes in investment projects and [3] China's domestic policy regarding national minorities." He politely but repeatedly concluded that "Insufficient attention to resolving these issues may slow down the process of projects implementation under the Chinese initiative in Central Asia in the future."

While "The absence of clear legislative regulations imposing liability for corruption when investing outside the country, in a short-term perspective puts the Chinese investor in a preferential position" and while "at the moment, Central Asian countries are open to Chinese investments, …the medium- and long-term success of the 'Belt and Road Initiative' implementation in Central Asia will depend on many factors that must be considered by the Chinese side and the countries of Central Asia – recipients of investments from the PRC." "Progress in the development of the 'Belt and Road Initiative' will depend on how far China can take action to solve the emerging problems and [for their part] Central Asian states also need to develop standards for cooperation with the PRC apart from economic indicators, pay[ing] more attention to environmental and social issues."

1. Sustainable Development: Environmental Modernization Issues

The growth of the Chinese economy, as in other industrializing countries, is accompanied by environmental problems. Studies show that environmental modernization within China, aimed at improving the environmental situation, was not reflected in the adjustment of investment activities outside the country. In addition, the governments in underdeveloped and developing countries often lower environmental standards to attract foreign investors, despite the fact that infrastructure projects (railways, roads, pipelines and power lines) usually carry risks of reducing biodiversity, change of ecosystem, and environmental pollution, during construction and exploitation.

For example, Tracy *et al.* (2017) stated it this way:

Concurrently, on the domestic front, the Chinese Government has launched a new policy paradigm, "ecological civilization," to dramatically improve environmental regulations, reduce pollution, and transform industries by adopting new green technologies and higher environmental standards. But does China's intention to go through a "green shift" domestically resonate with these new trans-border infrastructure development mega-projects?

If China has only recently begun to discuss environmental issues at the highest level and to take serious measures, is it worth expecting that Chinese investors will be more responsible for environmental issues in underdeveloped and developing countries? Risks in the implementation of the "Belt and Road Initiative" in Central Asia investments and for its own governments in terms of environmental safety are inevitable.

2. Chinese Investments and Domestic Policies of Recipient Countries

The absence of clear legislative regulations imposing liability for corruption when investing outside the country in a short-term perspective puts the Chinese investor in a preferential position…. But in the medium and long-term perspective, this strategy carries risks for Chinese investors, including in the framework of "Belt and Road Initiative." There are two reasons for risks.

First, there is a risk now to become an object of discontent on the part of the societies of recipient countries of investment. The existing sinophobic sentiments can be reinforced by the not-fully-responsible behavior of Chinese investors, which will create difficulties for the existing and future projects within the framework of "Belt and Road Initiative."

Secondly, regime change is always possible, and the new authorities might keep relations with China, but not share the enthusiasm of their predecessors. In Malaysia, after the defeat of the previous prime-minister Najib Tun Razak, accused of corruption, and the "Alliance of Hope" coalition came to power, the state policy regarding Chinese projects also changed. The new government has already suspended two projects under the "Belt and Road Initiative," The main reason [being] the increase in external debt.

"Environmental and other problems associated with Chinese investments, such as attracting illegal labor or using only Chinese materials, are not adequately addressed at this stage."

3. China's National Minority Policy and Investments in Central Asia

Central Asia is a key region for economic growth for Xinjiang and development of a land corridor between China and Western countries as an alternative to the sea routes.

In relations with the countries of Central Asia, one of the risk factors for the "Belt and Road Initiative" is the policy of the PRC regarding ethnic minorities in the Xinjiang Uighur Autonomous Region. Although issues of domestic policy and investment are often considered separately, in the case of China's policy on national minorities of the Xinjiang Uighur Autonomous Region…

Michael H. Glantz

it already has a negative impact on perception of China and "Belt and Road Initiative" by Central Asia. The mass media of Kazakhstan, broadcast in the Kazakh language, actively follow the processes in Xinjiang.

For the development of western China or Xinjiang, close cooperation with the countries of Central Asia, through which opens a land access to the markets of Russia, Iran and Europe, is very important. The developing Xinjiang also gets access to mineral resources in Central Asia. But in the past few years, an attempt to erase ethnic and religious identity and "sinification" of minorities can be seen in China's domestic policy towards national minorities in Xinjiang. (Kuo, 2018) What is happening does not quite correspond to the construction of a positive image of the PRC. The language of power, total control, the rejection of cultural diversity, an attempt to erase national identity, especially related to the societies of the peoples of Central Asia, creates an image of an aggressive neighbor. Will this lead to an increase in conflict or end in cultural genocide?

"For any outcome, this process negatively impacts the perception of China, not only in Central Asia but throughout the world. The discourse of hostility will significantly limit the possibilities for full-fledged economic cooperation. Given that, national minorities in China, including the Uighurs, Kazakhs and Kyrgyz, could be a bridge in creating closer and more sustainable economic ties."

Furukawa (2018) observed that "Moscow seems to tolerate China's growing clout in Russia's sphere of influence." However, he also noted some Chinese activities could eventually undermine its relationship with Russia because of its loans to the pro-West Ukraine and Moldova.

REFERENCES

 Cohen, A., 2018. "As Global Markets Cool, Investors Find Warmth in Central Asia's Infrastructure." GEO. Ariel Cohen & Associates (December 17).

 Cohen, A. and J. Grant, 2018. *Future Calling: Infrastructure Development in Central Asia – Unlocking Growth in the Heart of Eurasia.* International Tax and Investment Center, Issues Paper. Washington, DC (October).

 Durso, J., 2018. "Central Asia Opens Door to Afghanistan." *The Diplomat* (May 10).

 Furukawa, E., 2018. "Belt and Road debt trap spreads to Central Asia: China exploits rift between US and Russia to court Ukraine." *Nikkei Asian Review* (August 29).

 Idan, A., 2018. "China's Belt and Road Initiative: Relieving Landlocked Central Asia." *CACI Analyst* (May 1).

 Kuo, L., 2018. "'Sinicisation' of Muslims in Xinjiang must go on, says Chinese official." *The Guardian* (October 14).

 Moldashev, K., 2019. "Risks in the Implementation of the Belt and Road Initiative in Central Asia." *Academia* (Jan 11).

 Tracy E.F., E. Shvarts, E. Simonov and M. Babenko, 2017. "China's new Eurasian ambitions: the environmental risks of the Silk Road Economic Belt." *Eurasian Geography and Economics*, 58:1, 56-88.

A Russia-China eventual Great Game over Central Asia?

Focusing on Eurasia's New Great Game, Harper (2017) commented mainly on China and Russia. "The Belt and the Road Initiative (BRI) represents most recent [Chinese] engagement with the former Soviet Union. While China's involvement in the region has often been seen as a recent development, it is also the latest chapter of China's long history in Eurasia…. This history has played a role in shaping China's perception of its international role, which China views as the country's return to Great Power status rather than its rise." Harper also noted that "The BRI and other Chinese initiatives in the region pose as much of a threat to Russian interests as for Western concerns. While China and Russia have common security interests, there is the potential for clashes over economic initiatives, with fears that China may edge Russia out of its own sphere of influence."

According to Wilson (2016), "China has been actively building up its trade and investment partnerships in the republics of the Former Soviet Union." He also noted that:

> In 2013, trade between China and the five Central Asian states (Kazakhstan, Kyrgyzstan, Tajikistan, Turkmenistan and Uzbekistan) totaled $50 billion [USD], while the five states' trade with Russia – previously the region's top economic player – amounted to only $30 billion [USD].
>
> China has also redrawn Central Asia's energy economics. Their companies now own close to a quarter of Kazakhstan's oil production and account for well over half of Turkmenistan's gas exports. They also signed $15 billion [USD] in gas and uranium deals with Uzbekistan.

For its part, Russia's top trade partner is China. This could eventually lead to China's conflict over Russia's perceived national, political and economic spheres of influence.

These two neighbors share the common interest to reduce America's global influence, based on the belief that the enemy of my enemy is my friend: "Although the Chinese and Russians may not be natural economic allies due to historical grievances…expanded alliances between the two countries unfold if either presidential hopeful, particularly Donald Trump, acts on promises to get tough on China." (Hsu, 2016) As we now know, Trump has opened what almost all economists consider Pandora's box by launching a trade war with China and by continuing to escalate it (e.g., Swanson and Bradsher, 2018). At the same time, President Trump has continued to curry favor with Russia's Putin, despite the strong evidence of Russia's tampering with the 2016 US presidential election.

Nevertheless, "While the New Great Game appears to be a tripolar rivalry [with the third pole being the US], it would appear that it is increasingly becoming a Sino-Russian affair with only a somewhat diminished American presence in Eurasia." (Harper, 2017) Generally speaking, a balance of power among three countries is inherently unstable. If two states in a three-party balance of power choose to join together (in this case Russia and China) to successfully oppose the third party (in this case the United States), it would leave two states in an unstable alliance, because the stronger of the two could dominate, should it choose to do so. The two remaining countries in the alliance would eventually be in a competitive mode for dominant influence in the Central Asian countries, republics of the former Soviet Union that are viewed by Moscow as falling within both its geographic and functional spheres of influence, much in the same way Russia views the Ukraine's Crimea, and even the Ukraine itself.

Wilson (2018) suggested that whatever their relationship might appear to be at the moment, Russia and China are in an asymmetric relationship:

> The stark fact is that China is almost universally considered to be a rising power, while Russia is, at least in a relative sense, in a situation of decline. The

equilibrium of the interactions between the two states is also challenged by China's ambitions, under the leadership of Xi Jinping, to assume a leading voice on the world stage.

The asymmetry in their rivalry can also be seen in how they expand their respective spheres. Russia

Fig. 22   Russia-China cooperation: a win-win situation? *D. Parkins.*

region, China has become comfortable working with Central Asian countries bilaterally. At the same time, China launched new efforts like the Asian Infrastructure Investment Bank and the BRI that have enabled it to engage with Central Asia in multilateral fora outside of the SCO.

emphasizes institutional power as granted by intergovernmental organizations (IGOs) and multilateral agreements. Reflecting on the Shanghai Cooperation Organization (SCO), Foreign Policy Research Institute fellow Felix K. Chang (2018) provides an example:

> Broadly, Russia has attempted to put itself at the center of international bodies that span Eurasia. In 2015, Moscow brought three of them together at one time in the Russian city of Ufa: the annual SCO meeting, the annual BRICS summit, and an informal meeting of the Eurasian Economic Union (EAEU), a Russia-dominated economic union of former Soviet republics. At the SCO meeting, Russia revealed its true colors. Rather than push ahead with a Chinese proposal to create an SCO free trade area, which would likely have expanded not only trade, but also China's footprint across Central Asia, Russia demurred and argued that it needed time to reach a consensus within the EAEU first.

China is not particularly troubled by roadblocks of this manner. Rather than leaving its interests in the hands of international bodies, China forges bilateral agreements or entirely new IGOs. In Chang's (2018) words:

> Unfortunately for Russia, by the mid-2010s, China no longer felt the need to pursue its objectives in Central Asia through the SCO. Whereas China had once been conscious not to irritate Russia in the

This approach consistently undermines Russia's moves in the Great Game, breaking roadblocks down to speedbumps.

Wilson (2018) went on to say:

> The Kremlin is also acutely aware that the Chinese economic juggernaut poses a threat to Russia's perceived sphere of influence in the post-Soviet space, especially in Central Asia.

Aside from adverse speculation about their bilateral cooperation, there are positive win-win aspects. For example, Hsu (2016) reported that:

> One Belt One Road is an obvious opportunity for both China and Russia: China would provide Russia with much-needed investment and infrastructure, and Russia would build up sorely-needed infrastructure which could breathe some life into its lagging economy.

Russian-Chinese cooperation is also being strengthened in the Arctic region, as China asserts its rights to traverse Arctic waters as a self-declared "near Arctic" state. Like many governments, China seems to have no permanent friends or permanent enemies but it does have permanent interests, as was said about the British Empire in its heyday.

REFERENCES

 Chang, F., 2018. "Organization of Rivals: Limits of the Shanghai Cooperation Organization." Foreign Policy Research Institute (September 27).

 Harper, T., 2017. "BRI and the New Great Game in Eurasia." *CPI Analysis* (November 29).

 Hsu, S., 2016. "Is a Russia-China Economic Alliance on The Horizon?" *Forbes* (November 7).

 Swanson, A. and K. Bradsher, 2018. "Trump Doubles Down on Potential Trade War with China." *New York Times* (April 5).

 Wilson, W.T., 2016. "China's Huge 'One Belt, One Road' Initiative is Sweeping Central Asia." The Heritage Foundation. (November 21)

 Wilson, J.L., 2018. "The asymmetry of China-Russia relations." *Asia Dialogue* (UK) (March).

Michael H. Glantz

An emerging Polar Great Game: China's Polar Maritime Road

Eleven years ago, Russia's Putin took the surprising step of having a titanium Russian Federation flag planted on the Arctic's seabed to assert the country's sovereignty over its continental shelf. "Russia symbolically staked its claim to billions of US dollars' worth of oil and gas reserves in the Arctic Ocean today when two mini submarines reached the seabed more than two and half miles beneath the North Pole." (Parfitt, 2007) By doing so, Putin was taking advantage of the fact that human-induced greenhouse gas emissions are heating up the global climate, which is accelerating the melting of the Arctic sea ice. In decades, global warming will make mining of the seabed possible and will open up year-round ice-free Arctic waters to large scale cargo traffic.

The history of disappearing Arctic sea ice shows, according to researchers, that it has been accelerating and receding. Sea ice has a major feedback (reinforcing) influence on the warming of the atmosphere. With a reduction in the polar sea ice and snow cover (white) surface area which reflects incoming infrared radiation back to space, the darker surrounding water heats up. This means that the sea lanes in the Arctic will open up year-round so that ships carrying cargo from Asia to Europe or vice versa will cut the travel time by half, for example. Not only will the voyages be short in time but also a safer route. Boles (2018) wrote, "Beijing noted that, due to global warming, 'Arctic shipping routes are likely to become important routes for international trade.' Beijing says global warming means the route is navigable for longer periods – making it a modern version of the ancient Silk Road from East to West." China has already used the ice-free part of the Arctic a couple of times in the past five years. (Patel, 2017) However, as Babones (2018) observed:

> The Polar Silk Road will only be open in the summer for decades to come. Sea ice and vicious weather conditions will continue to make the winter journey too dangerous even as global warming

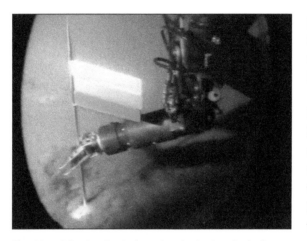

Fig. 23 A Russian flag is planted on the Arctic seabed to lay claim to the continental shelf and its resources. *Gautier de Blonde.*

progresses. From an environmental perspective, it may be too dangerous at any time.

People may be surprised to learn that China has been an observer state of the Arctic Council since 2013, coincidentally the same year the OBOR Initiative was launched. Although China does not border on the Arctic Ocean, it has proclaimed itself to be a "near Arctic state" (Hawksley, 2018), citing the UN convention on the Law of the Sea (UNCLOS) as its legal right to do so. It has called its Arctic-related development activities the Polar Silk Road.

Polar Silk Road

The Polar Silk Road has belatedly become a strategic concern to the US, having been discussed publicly in a US Senate Armed Services Committee hearing. More recently, Goodman and Freese (2018) wrote about a new US Naval strategy document for the Arctic, which was released in the summer of 2018:

> What the US Navy planned as a 16-year road map needs updates after only four years, in part due to receding polar ice caps, which are "opening new

trade routes, exposing new resources, and redrawing continental maps." But also, in part due to the rise of China as an "Arctic stakeholder," an increasing important player in the region.

Hawksley (2018) noted five key Chinese interests in the Arctic: (1) shipping routes will be opening up across the Arctic in the next few decades as a result of the adverse impacts of global warming reducing the extent of sea ice; (2) the Arctic region is believed to be resource-rich and the Chinese are preparing technologically for exploitation of those resources in the seabed and in the water column above it, directly and indirectly; (3) geopolitically, China has become very active, for example, in its militarization of the South China Sea and has allied with Russia on a range of geopolitical issues; (4) China has technology that Russia needs for its own exploitation of the Arctic's resources; (5) Close cooperation in the Arctic could lead to access of China's military fleet to ports on Russian territory. A key pillar of OBOR/BRI's infrastructure construction is building new, or upgrading existing, port infrastructure worldwide.

Brady (2018) takes China's interest and activities in

Fig. 24 The Polar Silk Road: China's trans-Arctic sea route in an ice-free Arctic Ocean. *CCB.*

polar regions to a new level with a forward-looking perspective in her book *China as a Polar Great Power.* A summary statement on the book's contents is as follows:

China has emerged as a member of the elite club of nations who are powerful at both global poles. Polar states are global giants, strong in military, scientific, and economic terms. The concept of a polar great power is relatively unknown in international relations studies; yet China, a rising power globally, is now widely using this term to categorize its aspirations and emphasize the significance of the polar regions to their national interests. China's focus on becoming a polar great power represents a fundamental re-orientation – a completely new way of imagining the world.

Christopher Layne wrote, "OBOR is a milestone on China's path to great power status and is one of several indicators of receding American power – not just geographically but also in matters involving the international economy and international institutions." (cited in Wilson, 2018)

REFERENCES

 Babones, S., 2018. "Even China's 'Polar Silk Road' Can't Change The Inconvenient Map Of Eurasia." *Forbes* (January 28).

 Boles, T., 2018. "Polar Silk Road: Chinese planning trade route through melting Arctic to halve travel time." *The Sun* (UK), (January 27).

 Brady, A-M., 2018. "China as a Polar Great Power." Cambridge University Press (February).

 Goodman, S. and E. Freese, 2018. "China's Ready to Cash in on a Melting Arctic." *Foreign Policy* (May 1).

 Hawksley, H., 2018. "China's Arctic plan spreads a chill." *Nikkei Asian Review* (February 16).

 Hui, L., 2018. "China's Arctic Policy." *Xinhuanet* (January 26).

 Parfitt, T., 2007. "Russia plants flag on North Pole seabed." *The Guardian* (August 2).

 Patel, J. and H. Fountain, 2017. "As Arctic Ice Vanishes, New Shipping Routes Open." *New York Times* (May 3).

A Great Game in Southeast Asia

China appears to be broadening and solidifying what it perceives to be within its sphere of influence (SOI) in the Southeast Asia. What is happening is yet another Great Game that involves the 10 members of the Association of Southeast Asian Nations (ASEAN), Australia and the United States. China is on a fast track to encompass in its SOI most, if not all, of ASEAN's Southeast Asian member states. The states that do not comply can become isolated.

Australian correspondent Layton (2017) wrote about his country's concern:

> In a "sphere of influence," the dominant state can constrain and guide the foreign and domestic policy choices of other states within a particular region without using direct military coercion. For China, establishing a Southeast Asian sphere of influence would bring it several benefits. In making regional states more pliable, China could gain implicit veto power over any unfavorable actions they might take. Regional states would become less willing to provide long-term basing to American forces or short-term support for transiting U.S. forces.
>
> The future seems obvious: Southeast Asia is steadily becoming part of China's sphere of influence. This process may be accelerated in the Trump era, as the administration seems so far to have little interest in the region. As U.S. power recedes, China appears ready to fill the gap. For Australia, Southeast Asia falling within China's sphere of influence would be a strategic catastrophe. Australia would be on the perimeter of Chinese power. It would be exposed, more isolated, and vulnerable to coercion and intimidation. (See also Darwin Port Dilemma, p. 95, below.)

This prospect has become unsettling to Australia and should be to the United States. China has had varied re-

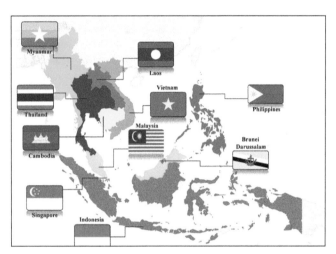

Fig. 25   ASEAN country members' motto: "One vision, One identify." *CCB*.

lations throughout history with the individual ASEAN member countries. Here we focus on the Association of Southeast Asia Nations (ASEAN). The Chinese diaspora throughout the region makes up a notable Chinese minority population in each of these countries. Environmentally, several countries are linked by major rivers, including the Mekong River, that begin their flow from China's Tibetan-Qinghai Plateau. Variations in streamflow in the lower reaches of these rivers have a great impact on lives and livelihoods in the lower Mekong River Basin.

Chow (2017) wrote an article entitled "China is weaponizing water," reporting on the environmental impacts on ASEAN communities and individuals, as a result of China's socio-economic and political influence and its water-related decisions.

> With the flip of a switch, the Middle Kingdom can release hundreds of millions of gallons of water from its mega dams, causing catastrophic floods that would reshape entire ecosystems in countries downstream…. In addition to floods, Chinese dams are also believed to be responsible for worsening droughts. Last year, Vietnam pleaded with China to release water from the Yunnan dam on the Mekong River to ease severe water shortages downstream. China agreed and waters flowed into Cambodia, Laos, Myanmar, Thailand and Vietnam. These two

extremes not only highlight the environmental impact of Chinese dams, but also serve as a stark reminder of China's influence over its southern neighbors.

China's regional activities at sea are exposed by its expansion and takeover in the South China Sea and by developing military bases on built-up reefs and artificial islands. Perhaps the next expansion of its desired regional SOI will encompass the entire geographic area covered by the ASEAN members.

OBOR/BRI is providing ASEAN countries funding for what the governments in the region need and want…infrastructure connectivity. China is offering through OBOR/BRI to overcome the region's infrastructure "financial deficit gap." This would enhance ASEAN's collective strength and political voice as a regional institution composed of relatively small states. A real concern, however, is that bilateral dependence on China through infrastructure loans to connect countries in Southeast Asia could weaken ASEAN's multilateral drive toward strengthening the region as a community. Providing development loans for infrastructure in the region is not a selfless act by Chinese authorities. For example, some of the high-speed rail lines will directly link Southeast Asian countries to China's landlocked Yunnan Province, giving China a direct gateway to seaports: Yunnan to Thailand's eastern coast and Yunnan's Kunming to Singapore, another major trade partner with China.

Fig. 26 Are ASEAN countries increasingly tethered to China? *A. Rae.*

Some ASEAN member state leaders are optimistic about the potential value of BRI projects in their countries. Projects such as a bullet train system in Laos and telecommunication improvements in Brunei have led to positive press stories from respective state leaders. (Xia, 2018) "The (BRI) will benefit many countries that need more and better infrastructure. It is also compatible with keeping the regional architecture and international system open and inclusive." The Prime Minister of Singapore offered a statement of support that recognizes the

potential economic benefits for Singapore, which could perhaps utilize the increased interconnectedness and infrastructure buildup provided by BRI. (Cheong, 2018)

However, a level of skepticism also remains as it relates to BRI and ASEAN ties. An editorial recently shared in the *ASEAN Post* (2018), entitled "Belt and Road buckles under own weight," sheds light on regional views about why China's projects will not lead to its future hegemony. Rather, BRI is a fragmented strategy which does not consider project quality. In addition, an overall lack of organization could ultimately doom the plan and recipient states, which could pose negative consequences for the ASEAN states, especially those which have welcomed BRI investments.

Another skeptical perspective from *Asia Times'* Benjamin Zawacki (2018) posits that the BRI, like other Chinese initiatives, is designed largely to "expand China's geo-political footprint in the region while checking those of the US, Japan, and Taiwan." The economic benefit of these projects is second to expanding China's sphere of influence, so disorganization and fragmentation are minor setbacks.

The stance toward China's BRI of countries in Southeast Asia is not just in terms of black or white, yes or no. Some countries express mixed feeling or have shown their mixed reactions to China's growing involvement in the region. Vietnam is a good example of such a cautionary response. Hiep (2018) provided a useful summary of his article on Vietnam's reactions to the BRI.

- Vietnam is offering diplomatic support to China's Belt and Road Initiative (BRI), but is cautious about applying for loans from it. This attitude can be explained by:
  ◦ Its distrust of Beijing and concerns about the strategic implications of the Initiative in the context of the South China Sea disputes;
  ◦ The unattractive commercial terms and conditions of Chinese loans; and
  ◦ Vietnam's access to other options.

- Hanoi may start by applying for a couple of "pilot" projects, especially through private investors, in order to get a better assessment of the BRI.
- Although the actual implementation of the BRI in Vietnam may be slow, there is little doubt that Hanoi will continue to lend diplomatic support to the Initiative.
- As the BRI is about China's stature as a benevolent rising power, Vietnam's diplomatic support for it will still matter to China.

Perhaps the most critical voice in the region is Malaysia. Malaysia's criticism of OBOR/BRI was in the spotlight in August 2018, when it cancelled two major projects with China over concerns regarding the resulting debt and general sustainability. (Erickson, 2018) In response, China's vice-finance minister claimed debt concerns would be "taken care of," despite the complex nature of BRI loan arrangements. Since then, Malaysia has stated its intentions of remaining in the Initiative (and to thoroughly vet all future deals) and China has remained respectful of Malaysia's wishes, perhaps hoping to assuage debt trap concerns by allowing each nation a full opportunity to evaluate their deals. (*Straits Times*, 2018) Malaysian media has continued to view the Initiative skeptically despite this, with *Astro Awani*'s Karim Raslan recently claiming 2018 as the year of the BRI's "failure," summarizing it as "we pay, they benefit." (Raslan, 2018)

As China's relationship with most ASEAN states continues to revolve around the potential for economic growth and shared potential via regional interconnectivity, BRI project failure has the potential to be a catalyst for increased regional tensions and negative economic outcomes. In many ways, the ASEAN-BRI intersections mirror those of many BRI recipient states. If China's theory holds with regard to the projects, recipient states may enjoy significant improvements, albeit at varying political costs. If, on the other hand, BRI projects collapse under their own weight and lack of planning and oversight, the ASEAN region could face major economic and political setbacks. ASEAN represents a comprehensive governing body that should theoretically act as somewhat of a regional "check" on unbridled Chinese hegemony.

Yet another perspective can make the argument that, as individual ASEAN countries become increasingly involved in BRI projects, the overall structure and function of the organization and its ability to react to Chinese influence can be weakened.

Singapore has been seen as a major player in implementing BRI projects in India, one of the strongest overall critics of the China's BRI actions to date. (Ryan, 2018) Singapore's role in BRI-related Indian development can be seen in projects like OneHub Chennai, in which Singapore led the development of an industrial zone with an Indian real estate organization and Japanese investors. Moreover, additional projects within India are slated to commence in the near future. (Ryan, 2018) Singapore's role in expanding BRI projects into India is an interesting example of state-based partnerships serving as workarounds for investment in BRI-resistant countries.

China's Malacca Strait Dilemma: What Does the Kra Canal Have to Do With It?

Southeast Asia's Malacca Strait is a highly trafficked marine pathway for cargo shipments between the Indian Ocean and the South China Sea. Though people have not seen it this way, China until recently perceived itself to be land-locked, encircled in a way by US allies (Japan, Taiwan, South Korea) and US-friendly Southeast Asian countries (e.g., the Philippines, Vietnam, Thailand, Australia, New Zealand). It was one of the key reasons that a Chinese political scientist in the early 2010s called on China's political leaders to "March West." President Xi's Silk Roads and Belts routes, generally speaking, went toward Western Europe indirectly as well as directly, ostensibly to increase trade.

China's actions in this decade to solidify control over its self-declared nine-dash line sphere of influence over the South China Sea has also been an attempt to take control of its economic future, as much of its trade crosses the Malacca Strait. Zawecki (2018) highlighted the great importance to China of the Malacca Strait:

Through the Strait passes nearly half the world's annual shipping fleet and two-thirds of its oil and liquefied natural gas. On a daily basis, Malacca receives three time greater the oil traffic of the Suez Canal and 15 times that of the Panama Canal.

He also noted that:

…no single nation is more dependent on the Malacca Strait than China whose two-way share of trade and energy in the channel exceeds the global aggregate – the result of lacking direct littoral access to the Indian Ocean…. And dependency is vulnerability in China's case, given that the Strait is patrolled and policed by the US Navy's Seventh Fleet.

Pookaman (2018) reported about an emerging aspect of China's Malacca dilemma:

The Malacca Strait is estimated to reach saturation in 2024 when more than 140,000 vessels seek to pass through the narrow waterway…. The Strait's narrowness reduces the sea lane…in width, making passing ships vulnerable to maritime accidents, piracy and terrorism.

There is one major resolution to the Malacca dilemma for China, a Kra Canal. Pookaman wrote that:

For 300 years, visionaries have thought of dredging a great canal 150km across the Kra Isthmus in southern Thailand so that vessels sailing from the Indian Ocean to the Pacific could cut hundreds of kilometers off their voyage and avoid the Bugis pirates of Indonesia that for centuries have haunted the Strait of Malacca…. The Thai [Kra] Canal would offer the shortest link between the Indian and Pacific Oceans compared to other routes.

The Kra Canal would be yet another pearl in OBOR/BRI's

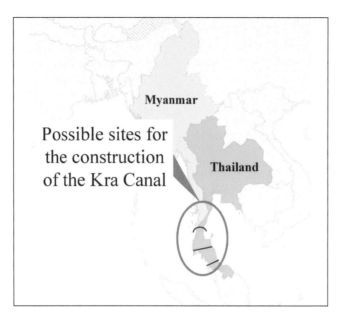

Fig. 27   Possible sites for the construction of the Kra Canal across the isthmus in Southern Thailand. *CCB.*

increasing maritime "string of pearls." But who will end up financing such a canal? Discussions are underway within Thailand and between Thailand and China. The backdrop to the discussions includes the following: "the belief that China has the funding and could easily link this to its BRI," China's militarization related to it maritime "string of pearls" and an opportunity for China's trade to circumvent the Malacca Strait obstacle as well as the growing pushback to China's OBOR/BRI loan arrangements in the region sparked by Sri Lanka's debt trap. (See Vietnam video *China's Great Game on Kra Canal*, SBS.com.au, 2018)

In addition, there are political and cultural problems for Thailand in the area where the Kra Canal would be constructed. Aside from environmental concerns, Menon (2018) mentioned two key problems: "The southern portion of the country (south of the proposed canal) has seen an increasing divide between Thai Buddhists and Thailand's Malay Muslims…. The construction of the Kra Canal would further exacerbate the volatile region, creating further divisions within the country." As of this writing, no final decision about constructing the canal and, if so, the loan arrangements, have been made. Menon noted that "apart from the Chinese interests in the region…the Thai government is trying to attract other international funding from Japan, South Korea, India, and ASEAN countries."

REFERENCES

 The ASEAN Post, 2018. "Belt and Road buckles under own weight." (September 28)

 Cheong, D., 2018. "Belt and Road Initiative a focal point for Singapore's ties with China." *The Strait Times* (April 8).

 Chow, E.K., 2017. "China is Weaponizing Water." *The National Interest* (August 26).

 Erickson, A. 2018. "Malaysia cancels two big Chinese projects, fearing they will bankrupt the country." *Washington Post* (August, 21).

 Hiep, L.H., 2018. *The Belt and Road Initiative in Vietnam: Challenges and Prospects.* ISEAS – Yusof Ishak Institute (Singapore), p. 2. (March 29).

 Layton, P., 2017. "As China's Sphere of Influence Expands, Australia has a Choice." *War on the Rocks*, University of Texas. (June 6).

Menon, R., 2018. "Thailand's Kra Canal: China's way around the Malacca Strait." *The Diplomat* (April 6).

 Pookaman, P., 2018. "Thailand's Kra Canal: Economic and Geopolitical Implications." *Asian Sentinel* (July 17).

 Raslan, K., 2018. "Ceritalah ASEAN – One year later, are the tables turning on China's Xi Jinping?" *Astro Awani* (December 20).

 Ryan, D., 2018. "Singapore: The Belt and Road's Gateway to India." *The Diplomat* (September 27).

 SBS, 2018. "China's Great Game on Kra Canal." SBS.com.au (February 12).

 Straits Times, 2018. "China says it will 'take care of' debt issues of BRI projects." *Straits Times* (October 13).

 Xia, L., 2018. "China Focus: Belt and Road Initiative widens China-ASEAN cooperation." *Xinhuanet* (September 14).

 Zawacki, B., 2018. "Thailand the missing link in China's Maritime Silk Road." *Asia Times* (November 9).

A Latin American Great Game?

Donald Trump's election to the US presidency in November 2016 created an unintended and serendipitous boost to the Latin American expansion of China's OBOR/BRI. The US election of 2016 had put into power a person whose strategic policies aggressively support American nationalism and isolationism, while explicitly rejecting globalization and multilateral decision-making for conflict resolution. Tang and Wong (2016) summed up the impacts of the US election in the following way:

> With US president-elect Donald Trump threatening to build a wall on the Mexican border and force Asian allies to increase defense spending, Beijing is busy luring countries across the eastern hemisphere into its orbit, and then successfully so in the western hemisphere.

Fig. 28 The demise of the TPP in 2017 at the hands of the Trump administration. *P. Schrank, Economist.*

President Trump's isolationist tweets and policy pronouncements, and especially his outright verbal attacks on American allies, are stimulating policy shifts by current US allies and trade partners toward China. Trump's foreign policy advisors were slow to come to the realization that the OBOR/BRI-related advancements could be a serious threat to America's strategic interests.

As examples, Germany's Chancellor Angela Merkel said that Europe could no longer rely on the US for its defense and France's President Macron has proposed that Europe build up its own defense as a step toward European unification and autonomy from a sole reliance on the US for its own defenses.

Before Trump's election victory, President Obama had been fostering American involvement in the Trans-Pacific Partnership (TPP), a circum-Pacific Rim trade region that involved eleven other countries. Proponents argued that the TPP would open up new markets and enhanced trade in American goods and services. However, in the 2016 presidential election, both US presidential candidates Hillary Clinton and Donald Trump opposed US participation in the TPP, arguing that its passage would lead to manufacturing job losses in the US. On Trump's first day as president, in January 2017, he announced that the US was withdrawing from the TPP. For its part, China had been concerned about the TPP, because of the expected increase of US involvement in Asian markets. Now China had an open field to enhance its trade and infrastructure development activities, even though the other eleven country-members of the TPP decided to go forward without US participation.

Contrary to popular – and expert – expectations, the 11 remaining countries that would have participated in the original TPP along with the US chose to continue to work together in a Comprehensive and Progressive Agreement for Trans-Pacific Partnership (CPTPP). Their collaborative effort went into force December 31, 2018 for a subset (also called the vanguard) of the 11 countries: Japan, Singapore, Mexico, Australia, Canada, New Zealand. The remaining five countries are expected to ratify the agreement in early 2019: Vietnam, Malaysia, Peru, Chile and Brunei. Yet others have expressed interest in joining: Thailand, Taiwan, Indonesia, Colombia and even the UK. Pappenfuss (2018) noted the CPTPP "will slash tariffs across much of the Pacific Rim region – but not for the US since Trump administration officials pulled out of negotiations last year." The title of a British article by Evans-Pritchard (2018) captured a new political reality: "Pacific states launch bold trade pact, shaping world order as America retreats." He went on to suggest that "the world's most radical trade pact has come into force across the Pacific as the US sulks on the sidelines, marking a stunning erosion in American strategic leadership." Ironically, Evans-Pritchard wrote that "The latest twist is that Chinese officials have begun to explore the possibility of joining the pact that was supposed to exclude them...."

Morales and Gordon (2016) made the following observation about China's interest in the Western Hemisphere:

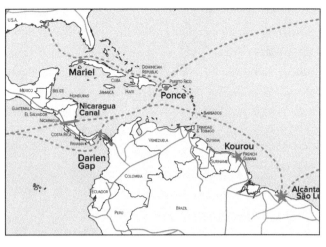

Fig. 29 OBOR/BRI financed deep-water ports in the Caribbean. *Schiller Institute.*

This would include building major projects in hurricane-ravaged Puerto Rico, including in Ponce on the southern coast of Puerto Rico, which could become a major port and shipping point for the Maritime Silk Road. Building a deep-water port there would open the whole transport corridors into the Gulf and East coasts of the United States. Connected with that, the Maritime Silk Road would do something similar in Mariel, Cuba, where there is also the plan to build a deep-water port. And since this is very close to the United States, it should all really be integrated into one big project.

International politics, even more than nature, abhors a vacuum. And with America's apparently headlong withdrawal from the Trans-Pacific Partnership (TPP) and metaphorically – if not yet physically – walling itself from Latin America, it is hardly surprising that Chinese-led alternatives were broached at the recent Asia-Pacific Economic Cooperation summit in Lima.

China had been engaged in bilateral development assistance for infrastructure in Latin America well before the OBOR/BRI initative was launched in 2013, such as for dam construction and mining in Ecuador. (Ministerio de Relaciones, 2016) It also has a bilateral agreement with Bolivia to provide military assistance. The *Latin American Herald Tribune* (*LAHT*, 2016) reported that "In July 2016, China donated 31 armored vehicles...to the Bolivian Armed Forces as part of a military cooperation program, which the Bolivian Government considers the most important. The program has also included training courses for Bolivian military personnel." The article went on to note, "At the meeting, the Chinese minister stressed that his country 'is willing to take military relations with Bolivia to a new level'."

As opposed to an expectable demand for a strong American competitive response to China's active "invasion" into what had been considered historically the US sphere of influence, a politically conservative US think tank (Zepp-Larouche, 2018) surprisingly proposed that "The U.S. Must Join China's Belt and Road in Developing the Caribbean And Central America." In a Schiller Institute video it suggested that:

Cuban authorities have actively been proposing a silk belt and road relationship with China for a few years. Cuba is offering itself as a Chinese beachhead in the Western Hemisphere for China's infrastructure development and trade enhancement in the Central America and Caribbean region and in South America. A Cuban official said that his nation "wanted to become a 'hub' of maritime and air transport in the region, namely through the Mariel Special Development Zone. This goal of our country can link us with China's Belt and Road Initiative and its purpose of extending this project to the Caribbean and Latin America." (*Xinhua*, 2017b)

Shi (2018) reminded readers, "As the US president drafts a $1-trillion [USD] plan to overhaul America's aging roads and bridges, Xi's infrastructure-building endeavor is pushing into the US backyard." To date, no such US domestic infrastructure plan has been forthcoming, but Chinese activities throughout Latin America have continued to increase unabated. All this has been going on in the Western Hemisphere, despite the US government officials' warnings and threats to Western Hemisphere countries about the dangers of their involvement with China and its OBOR/BRI loans, loans which are being labeled as "potential debt traps."

Construction of the Coca Codo Sinclair dam by Ecuador and China appears to be an example of a Western Hemisphere debt trap in the offing. To pay for this dam, the previous government of President Correa agreed to pay for its construction with oil exports to China. As much as 90% of oil taken from the ground was to go toward paying down the country's debts to China. In a recent article, Casey and Krauss (2018) wrote about the critical shortcomings of the dam stating that even if the dam does not work as designed, as expected or because of its use of low quality steel and other materials, China will still get paid for it. They wrote that "A giant dam was supposed to help lift Ecuador out of poverty. Instead, it's part of a national scandal, and future tethered to China." Unable to meet its loan obligations, Ecuador has been seeking financial assistance from Western banking institutions. At the same time it has sought to renegotiate the terms for paying back the Chinese banks.

Goodman (2016) wrote in his article entitled "As Trump talks wall, China builds bridges to Latin America" that "Nobody in the region is expecting much from Trump in terms of really productive policy. That leaves room for China to play a much more important role."

China's response to Trump-era policies of isolationism exposes an as-yet-unexpressed fact of life. Friedman (2017) reported on a previously unspoken fact of life expressed in 2013 by President Obama's Secretary of State John Kerry at a meeting with Latin American diplomats. Kerry remarked, "the era of the Monroe Doctrine is over." In case there were any lingering doubts about the fate of the Doctrine, those doubts were erased in 2017 by President Trump's America First policy, and his administration's other isolationist policies.

The new Silk Road is the purest illustration of Beijing's budding influence, as Washington is consumed with partisan bickering and fumbles for a coherent foreign policy. (Campbell, 2017) That fumbling continued worldwide into 2019.

Though many loans from China's AIIB have been in Asia, the AIIB plans to take the geographic expansion of OBOR/BRI to other continents. Kynge (2018b) reported in his article "AIIB set to extend reach to Latin America and Africa" that:

> The China-led AIIB is set to extend its financial operations to Latin America and Africa after reaching agreements with those regions' leading development banks. The moves represent an important step in the AIIB's metamorphosis from an Asia-focused lender

Fig. 30 The Monroe Doctrine's symbolic tombstone. *CCB.*

into a global institution similar in structure to the World Bank…. The move to co-finance with the IADB coincides with a clutch of Latin American countries joining the [AIIB]…. While Brazil was among 57 founding members, six other countries – Argentina, Chile, Ecuador, Bolivia, Peru, and Venezuela – are in the process of joining.

China has been involved in Latin American development projects for several years but, with the advent of the OBOR/BRI Initiative, its infrastructure activities are expected to increase sharply, as are its related trade agreements. The Latin American Great Game between China and the United States appears to be heating up. What follows are two examples, Venezuela and Argentina.

Venezuela and China: A 'Win-Win' or a Lose-lose' Partnership?

Ever since Hugo Chavez became president of Venezuela in 1999, China has been increasingly engaged in developing a relationship with the country's leftist governments. Ferchen (2018) wrote:

> It is certainly no coincidence that the majority of the loans were signed when Venezuela was led by Hugo Chavez. He offered an enticing diplomatic and even ideological partnership at a time when Chinese policy makers were looking at enhanced ties with Latin America as an opportunity to balance the United States' "pivot" to Asia.

Despite the "on again, off again" financial arrangements with China, the Venezuelan economy had been in trouble under Chavez and more recently and more seriously under Maduro's dictatorship, despite the fact that the country holds very large oil reserves on which the government has become overly dependent. What started well as a win-win proposition (infrastructure development for loans or for specific resources such as oil, gold, copper, etc.) before OBOR was launched in 2013 has turned into an apparent "lose-lose" situation for China. Venezuela's political system and economy have been hit by a perfect storm, with a sustained major drop in oil prices from its previous high-water mark, coupled with mismanagement of the oil industry and the economy, and corruption.

Balding (2017) reported that between 2007 and 2014, China provided over $60 billion US dollars in loans to the Venezuelan regimes in this decade in return for oil and mineral resources. In this period over 50 percent of China's loans to Latin America were with Venezuela. In that time frame, however, the setting for their relationship changed a lot. Maduro became president in 2013, following the death of Chavez. Oil prices worldwide fell to new lows from record-setting highs. Xi Jinping became China's leader and launched his OBOR Initiative. Trump, became US president in 2017 and pursued a nationalistic (anti-globalization) foreign policy. Maduro became increasingly dictatorial, as the economy of Venezuela suffered greatly.

By 2018, what had started out as a sweetheart deal (i.e., oil for infrastructure loans) turned into a perverse economic relationship between these countries, meaning that China continues to provide loans to an unpopular, undemocratic and corrupt government that has been on the edge of insolvency under Maduro's mis-rule.

China's *modus operandi*, through its OBOR Initiative, has been one of silence about the domestic issues of its OBOR partners. Balding (2017) noted that:

Officially, lending from Beijing comes without strings or concerns about non-financial matters. The reality is more nuanced. No one doubts Beijing cares little for niceties such as human rights, environmental protection, and anti-corruption when working abroad. Until recently, even geopolitical flag planting was relatively unimportant to Chinese technocrats.

The one possible payoff for China, financial benefits aside, would be if defaults on the loans to Maduro could lead to the establishment of a China-managed (if not controlled) deep-water port in Venezuela that could also serve strategically as a naval military base in the Western Hemisphere. For example, a Chinese-managed port at Venezuela's Puerto Cabello, 200 miles west of Caracas, would provide China the opportunity to exert influence not only for shipping but also for geopolitics in the strategic Gulf of Mexico.

Venezuela is one of the hemisphere's most repressed and desperate countries. Citizens struggle to meet their daily needs and are struggling to find employment. (Rogan, 2018) In July, China provided a stop-gap lifeline to Maduro with a $5 billion USD loan to increase oil exports to China. (Slav, 2018) The loan, however, is not enough to stimulate the country's economy by providing workers for the new oil extraction facilities.

China's loans help to keep the Maduro government in power, against all odds and apparently against the wishes of the people. Dyer (2018) reported that "some Venezuelans fear Maduro is selling them out to China." It is highly probable that once the Maduro regime has been ousted, the Venezuelan opposition, in accordance with its existing laws, would likely default on its loans to China. This is a perfect "lose-lose" relationship.

As another recent example of the emerging US-China conflict in the Central America and Caribbean region, as the *Latin American Herald Tribune* (*LAHT*, 2018) reported on the US Government response to the "encroachment" of Chinese influence in Central America, was when El Salvador terminated its diplomatic recognition of Taiwan in favor of diplomatic recognition of China.

The El Salvadoran government's receptiveness to China's apparent interference in the domestic politics of a western hemisphere country is of grave concern to the United States, and will result in a re-evaluation of our relationship with El Salvador," White House press secretary Sarah Sanders said in a statement…. "[T]his is a decision that affects not just El Salvador, but also the economic health and security of the entire Americas region.

The US reaction could be considered to be "a day late and a dollar short," as El Salvador joined a host of Latin American countries that had already established diplomatic and trade relations with China.

In sum, Nordin and Weissmann (2018) observed that "it is clear that Trump's approach to foreign policy has presented a window of opportunity for China, which Beijing has used skillfully to promote its claim to international leadership." (p. 249)

Argentina as a Functional Silk Road in America's Backyard

In 2015 China quietly negotiated a bilaterlal 50-year land-lease agreement for the construction and operation of a satellite tracking and space station antenna in a remote part of Argentina's Patagonia desert. Ostensibly, the space station, now built and operational, was to support a Chinese space shot to the dark side of the moon, a first attempt by any nation with a space program. At the time, this agreement was seemingly good for Argentina, given its chronic economic, including currency, volatility problems. In fact, China had come to the country's financial rescue several times since 2000.

This occurred during a period of indifference by the Western Hemisphere's dominant power, the United States. The apparent indifference, by both Democratic and Republican political administrations in America, to the economic woes of Argentina, as well as those of several other Latin American countries, created a perfect opening for President Xi's "going out" policy and for his Belt and Road Initiative. The most recent US indifference, under President Trump's isolationist and anti-immigration policies, has been viewed as America's active pursuit of disengagement policies from its hemispheric neighbors. As an after-thought, once the secret arrangement between China and Argentina had been exposed, as a result of political pressure from various groups within the country, the Government of Argentina convinced the Chinese to add to its original agreement that the space complex would not be used for military purposes. However, as is the case with China's deep-sea port construction around the globe (e.g., Djibouti; Sri Lanka, Pakistan), commercial ports and associated free trade zones can easily be used for military purposes.

Only recently, the US intelligence community has shown explicit concern about this Space Control Center in the Western Hemisphere, because it has the potential to track US transmissions and could in theory become useful to China to destroy working satellites of other countries.

For the US Government, it is yet again "a day late, and a dollar short," as the saying goes, because China has firmly planted itself in the hemisphere through trade, and economic and military aid to several countries. As suggested by Londoño (2018), "Beijing in Argentina is symbolic of the end of US dominant influence in the hemisphere." The Monroe Doctrine, declared in 1823 making the US the hemispheric hegemon, as noted earlier, is dead.

Latin countries, one by one over the years, have fallen into the Chinese functional sphere of influence through commercial as well as military trade, loans and other forms of timely infrastructure construction assistance. As Londoño reported (2018):

> The isolated base is one of the most striking symbols of Beijing's long push to transform Latin America and shape its future for generations to come – often in ways that directly undermine the United States' political, economic and strategic power in the region.

Durden (2018), after a review of Londoño's *New York Times* article noted above, ended his review with the following observation:

> Perhaps, in what would be a nightmare scenario for Western officials who've been caught off guard, China has indeed already staked out a new massive intelligence-collecting outpost south of America's border under the guise of space exploration.

REFERENCES

 Balding, C., 2017. "Venezuela's Road to Disaster is Littered with Chinese Cash." *Foreign Policy* (June 6).

 Campbell, C., 2017. "Ports, Pipelines and Geopolitics: China's New Silk Road is a Challenge for Washington." *TIME* (October 23).

 Casey, N. and C. Krauss, 2018. "It doesn't matter if Ecuador Can Afford This Dam. China Still Gets Paid." *New York Times* (December 19).

 Durden, T., 2018. "China To Take Over Kenya's Largest Port Over Unpaid Chinese Loan." Zero Hedge (December 27).

 Dyer, E., 2018. "Why some Venezuelans fear Maduro is selling them out to China." *CBC News (Canada)*. (September 15).

 Evans-Pritchard, A., 2018. "Pacific states launch bold trade pact, shaping world order as America retreats." *The Telegraph - Business* (December 30).

 Ferchen, M., 2018. "China, Venezuela, and the Illusion of Debt-Trap Diplomacy." *AsiaGlobal Online*, Carnegie-Tsinghua Center for Global Policy (Beijing) (August 16).

 Friedman, M.P., 2017. "Return of the Monroe Doctrine: Making Latin America Irate Again." *AULABLOG* (February 2).

Goodman, J., 2016. "As Trump talks wall, China builds bridges to Latin America." *Associated Press* (November 18).

 Kynge, J., 2018b. "AIIB set to extend reach to Latin America and Africa." *Financial Times* (May 7).

 LAHT, 2016. "China and Bolivia Discuss an Increase in Bilateral Military Cooperation." *Latin American Herald Tribune* (December 29).

 LAHT, 2018. "US to Review Relationship with El Salvador after Its Break with Taiwan." *Latin American Herald Tribune* (August 25).

 Londoño, E., 2018. "From a Space Station in Argentina, China Expands Its Reach in Latin America." *New York Times* (July 28).

 Ministerio de Relaciones Exteriores y Movilidad Humana, 2016. "Ecuador and China strengthen political, economic and commercial and investment relations." Republica del Equador (December 18).

 Morales, J.J. and P. Gordon, 2016. "China's belt and road can take its cues from the world's first model of globalisation." *South China Morning Post* (December 2).

 Nordin, A.H.M. and M. Weissmann, 2018. "Will Trump make China great again? The belt and road initiative and international order." *International Affairs*, Volume 94, Issue 2, March 2018, Pages 231–249.

 Pappenfuss, M., 2018. "Hard-Pressed American Farmers Left Out in The Cold By New 11-Nation Trade Treaty." *Huffington Post* (December 29).

 Rogan, T., 2018. "What if China sets up a naval base in Venezuela?" *Washington Examiner* (September 14).

 Shi, T., 2018. "China's Infrastructure Push Reaches Arctic, Leaving Out the U.S." *Bloomberg Quint* (January 29).

 Slav, I., 2018. "China Throws Venezuela's Oil Industry A $5B Lifeline." *Oil Price* (July 4).

 Tang, F. and C. Wong, 2016. "As Trump retreats, Xi Jinping moves to upgrade China's global power play." *South China Morning Post* (December 2).

 Xinhua, 2017b. "Cuba seeks to increase trade, join China's Belt and Road Initiative: official." *Xinhuanet* (November 1).

 Zepp-Larouche, H., 2018. "The U.S. Must Join China's Belt and Road In Developing The Caribbean and Central America." International Scholler Institute (January 16).

Great Game(s) in "Greater" Europe

The apparent original goal of the initiative was to use the ancient Silk Road as a symbol to expand and to heighten the quality as well as the volume of trade between Chinese provinces and Western Europe. Europe and the European Union, however, are not political, ideological or economic monoliths. They are composed of regions, as well as countries, at different levels of economic development, industrialization, political stability, and needs and wants. China has approached Europe "in parts" with regard to its One Belt One Road Initiative: northern, northwestern, central, eastern, southern and southeastern Europe.

Because China looks at Europe not as a unit but as sub-regional components, it has the option to approach European countries either multilaterally or, more often than not, bilaterally: country by country; and port by port. Aside from paying lip service to multilateralism, China's OBOR/BRI appears to thrive on bilateral negotiations with its potential partners. Bilateral agreements allow for less transparency, restrict bidding on projects by non-Chinese parties, and allow for free-wheeling and deal-making on a loan's conditions.

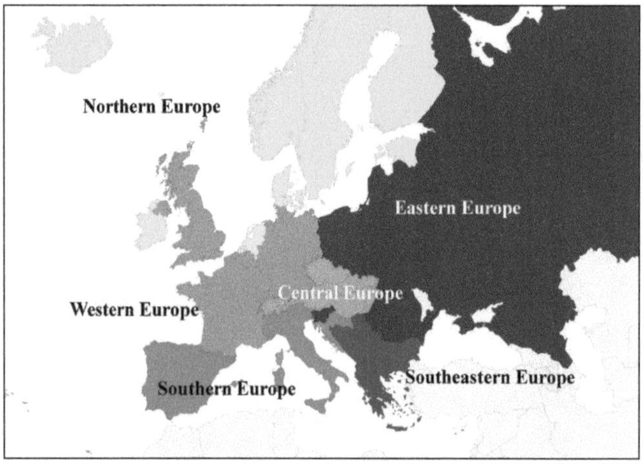

Fig. 31 Greater Europe's sub-regions are fair game for China's loans. *CCB*.

While some countries are skeptical about China's "win-win" slogan behind its OBOR/BRI loans for infrastructure, others trust in its "win-win" strategy. Reality lies in-between and varies by sub-regions within a Greater Europe. There are examples where the development loan conditions are being met. There are also situations where drastic actions (but legitimate according to the terms of the infrastructure loans) have been taken by China, when the borrower cannot meet its loan payments. The latter situation, in retrospect, has been referred to as a "debt trap," or as "debt-trap diplomacy." For example, China's loan to construct the Sri Lankan deep-water port of Hambantota has become the proverbial poster child for a debt trap, as it is now legally under the control of China for the next 99 years! Another debt trap example is Djibouti's major dependence on China due to its loan default. Yet other examples of loan defaults include a Chinese-constructed Kenneth Kaunda International airport in Zambia, as well as an airport in Sri Lanka.

These so-called debt traps are far from Europe distance-wise but are now part of an emerging early warning to prospective OBOR/BRI partners in western, eastern, central, southern and southeastern Europe to beware of the "smiling dragon." When a dragon's mouth is open, it is hard to know if it is smiling to greet you or getting ready to eat you!

European countries are not opposed to China's OBOR/BRI. However, they do want China to open up its process to their companies to be able to bid competitively on their oversease infrastructure projects. To date, most of the OBOR/BRI contracts have been with Chinese companies, which is considered by Europeans as an unfair business practice and counter to EU principles, if not regulations. China claims that it will open up the bidding process eventually. An "opening up" of the process would require transparency in its business arrangements, something that China has so far managed to avoid.

European businesses also want access to China's domestic markets, which China continues to protect. It is

Michael H. Glantz

easier for China to enter European markets than the other way around. In large measure, that is generally why most European governments oppose unfettered manufacturing acquisitions and access to their high-tech corporations and markets by Chinese firms that are backed financially by a government with seemingly deep pockets.

The debate over China's OBOR/BRI infrastructure loans or takeovers in Europe pit the richer, more industrialized Western European states against the relatively poorer southern, eastern, central and southeastern states that are in need of connectivity through new or refurbished infrastructure. A most recent political example of what might happen to the EU and its leadership's desire to speak with "one" voice is an unreleased report prepared by the 28 European ambassadors in Beijing. Hungary and Greece represent two such cracks in the EU wall of unity (see quote below). Hungary had received considerable Chinese loans for transportation infrastructure and Greece had received considerable Chinese loans much earlier to make its port of Piraeus a Chinese-controlled major gateway to Europe. In a key EU document to limit China's access to European markets, Hungary was the only country to refuse to sign a report agreed to by the other 27 EU ambassadors calling for the EU to restrict China's bilateral tactics in Greater Europe. (Prasad, 2018)

Martin (2018) highlighted the importance of the same report which had been leaked to the German business daily, *Handelsblatt*:

> The diplomats [28 European ambassadors in Beijing] cautioned that the $900 billion USD mega infrastructure project "runs counter to the EU agenda for liberalizing trade and pushes the balance of power in favor of subsidized Chinese companies…. [D]iplomats detailed this frustration at the lack of opportunities for European firms from the new Silk Road initiative."

As another sign of growing concern about Chinese influence inside the EU, Greece opposed an EU statement challenging China's human rights abuse record, and was the only dissenting country (27 to 1). The degree to which those opposing votes were linked to their governments' infrastructure loans from China seems obvious. Greece went public with its response to criticism by noting that it was following its national interests first and foremost, not EU interests. *OBOReurope* (2018b) reported the following: "Since the acquisition of Piraeus port by [China's] COSCO Company, in August 2016, Greece has become

a major stopover along the new silk roads. Athens aims at strengthening its position as the main Mediterranean gateway to the new Silk Roads in Europe." In August 2018 Greece officially joined the BRI.

Sheikh (2018) wrote that "Chinese loans are…to serve as Chinese footsteps in Europe through which Beijing will seek to build its influence. This is worrying for countries like Germany because it would ultimately allow China to use its presence in Eastern Europe to reach Western Europe and the EU at large." The warning for Europe, cited by Sheikh, is the following:

> As far as investment in infrastructure projects is concerned, it is no different from what China has been doing in Asia and Africa as loans that are typically well above the World Bank's level, and often, as in Pakistan and Sri Lanka, for instance, result in Chinese hegemonism. As *Asia Sentinel* has reported, Chinese infrastructure development of those countries has virtually turned them into vassal states owing billions in high-interest loans for projects that primarily benefit China to the detriment of the host country.

The importance of the word "One" appeared again, when the German Foreign Minister recently "called on Beijing to respect the concept of 'one Europe' adding: 'If we do not succeed for example in developing a single strategy toward China, then China will succeed in dividing Europe.'"

Although reluctant to join blocs with other governments, China joined central, eastern, southern and southeastern Europe to form the 16+1 group (China being the +1). Sheikh (2018) noted, "Eleven countries in the 16+1 are EU members, and there is concern that attempts to "bilateralize" relations in this framework could affect the internal cohesion of the EU and risk divisions among members that compete for Chinese attention."

In a book-length Conference report on 16+1 Cooperation, Xin (2018) provided insight into China's bilateral activities ever since the 1950s in the now-former socialist states of Central and Eastern Europe. He provided a brief history of China's relationship with Central and Eastern European (CEE) countries, noting that their relationship took hold in 2011 and the first Economic and Trade Forum was organized in Hungary in July 2018. The editor of the report wrote of his awareness of the concern in western European countries about China's strengthening relationship through OBOR/BRI infrastructure projects with this part of a Greater Europe:

China treats each country equally in Europe…. 16+1 Cooperation shows that China not only develops relations with west European countries, but also has the interest to develop relations with CEE countries as well…. When China is developing a close relationship with Germany, France and UK, takes high level meetings, signs economic and trade contracts, everybody [is] happy and nobody in these countries says it would divide and rule Europe. But when the 16+1 Cooperation develops, the voices from these [western] countries accuse (that) China would divide and rule the Europe.

Writing on the political situation, Richet (2018) in his contribution to the conference report highlighted one specific question among others. He wrote:

China's growing presence in the region raises the question of its influence on the countries of the region. Does China offer a plausible alternative to member[s] or acceding countries challenging the European order…, the methods of accession (Balkan countries), does its presence influence the political choices of certain countries on sensible subjects ultimately threatening the unanimity of the European Union's positions. (p. 7)

Richet (p. 10) included the following map in his paper, which clearly demarcates a potential sphere of influence for China.

He then mentioned China's two-track approach to western European markets:

[The CSEE] is both a gateway, a market of almost 100 million consumers, a springboard to the EU-15, and a part of Europe where infrastructure needs are great. A passage first of all. Poland to the overland route from Belarus [and] in southern Europe, the sea route, via the Suez Canal, reaches the port of Piraeus in Greece.

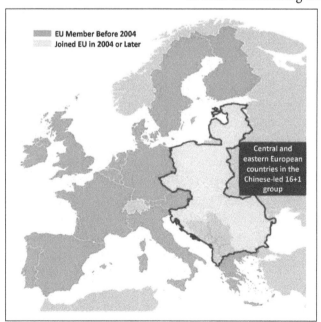

Fig. 32   China's sphere of influence in Europe? *CEE Institute.*

Such a Chinese foothold on the Greater European continent could prove to be a challenge to the European Union's ability to speak with one voice on various economic or political issues.

The latest crack to appear in European unity is Italy, the only G-7 member to sign a Memo of Understanding with China for infrastructure-related development assistance. Italy is considered one of the poorer countries, relatively speaking, and is in the southern tier of the continent along with Greece, Spain and Portugal. China is very interested in developing the port of Trieste, which once served as the Austro-Hungarian Empire's only direct outlet to the sea. Through this MOU, China can provide another beachhead in access to Western European markets for distribution of its goods and services. Girardi (2018) wrote that China has targeted Trieste, writing that "One port in the north of the Mare Nostrum [the Mediterranean] is now at the center of Beijing's interests for its geographic position, its connectivity with the rest of Europe and its strategic spot in the supply chain. It is the port of Trieste in northern Italy."

Girardi gathered statements from various Italian development authorities that show they are aware of problems to avoid in dealing with China's Belt and Road Initiative:

Chinese investors will fund the construction of new terminals, docks and platforms, as well as the modernization and expansion of the industrial area surrounding the port and the rail system that will deliver Chinese merchandise all over Europe.

Rome is welcoming Beijing's investors to extend the Belt and Road program to the European country by participating in sectors like railways, airlines and harbors. Italy's infrastructure has long been in crisis….

Italy is not Greece and will not end up in the debt trap that this kind of heavy investment could trigger.

The common worry

within European governments that fear a growing dependence of those countries is that, after taking money from Beijing, they will be pressured to align policies with the People's Republic.

Martin (2018), citing a Mercator Institute researcher, noted that "China has already succeeded on several occasions in undermining EU cohesion."

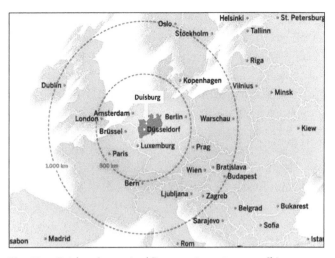

Fig. 33 Duisburg's perceived European importance, as China sees it. *CCB*.

Chinese goods, as BRI continues its sprawl throughout the West. Utilizing a rail hub like Duisburg will allow for a more efficient supply chain, and perhaps a connecting point for investments being made in other Eastern and Central European states.

One potential roadblock for such a grand rail plan is the "red tape" associated with operating trains between Europe and Asia. Posaner noted, "In one example of the costs of paperwork, negotiating passage for a trial Eurasian mail train across the Polish-Belarusian border added a day to transit times, according to the Intergovernmental Organization for International Carriage by Rail." (Posaner, 2018) However, it appears that progress in relations between China and Germany is being made, as travel times have decreased significantly since the trains started operations. The ultimate goal is for a Eurasian rail trip to take about a week. (Posaner, 2018)

An important anecdote is the perceived benefits of the Chinese trains. The mayor of Duisburg has proudly referred to the city as "China city," and has touted the economic benefits of the trains. (Oltermann, 2018) It is important to take into consideration the economic depression of Duisburg, which still has an extremely high unemployment rate. Many believe further Chinese-powered jobs could be created by weakening the power of the German labor unions. (Oltermann, 2018)

The case of Duisburg also offers a perspective of what can happen to cities within "developed" countries that have been neglected or ignored. If the choice is between unemployment or welcoming Chinese industry as a business partner, it is not difficult to understand why China's presence in the region is rapidly increasing, a trend that seems unlikely to stop in the absence of nationalistic or EU-related policy changes.

Is Duisburg, Germany an Example of China's Creeping Involvement in Europe?

An interesting case study is that of Duisburg, a former "rust belt" city in Germany that experienced a relative decline in prosperity as the global economy modernized. Recently, however, the city found itself as a central piece of evidence for China's increasing investment and subsequent involvement on the European continent. After all, one of BRI's focal points was the developing nations in Europe. What makes the case of Duisburg unique and interesting is its location within a "developed" country. It would appear to be too aware to engage with China's high risk and high interest rate investment projects.

According to Posaner (2018), however, Duisburg is an ideal location for Chinese investment, as a hub for rail transit and the supply chain between Chinese factories and European destinations. *Politico* reported, "Duisburg has become by far the most important hub in Europe for Chinese trains," said Erich Staake, CEO of the city's port.

"[On] every map you see in China there are two cities illustrated for Germany: Berlin and Duisburg – very often Duisburg is printed a little bit bigger." (Posaner, 2018) Geographically, Duisburg represents an ideal location because it is one of the only "distribution hubs" of Chinese goods and manufacturing located within the European continent. Furthermore, its central location within Germany would allow Chinese rail companies, often operated by German and European entities, to distribute materials, products, and goods from Duisburg throughout Europe. (Posaner, 2018) This plan ties into the overall BRI framework by acting as a further distribution source for

News Flash
EU's Italian Dilemma?

In early March, multiple news agencies reported that Italy and China engaged in advanced discussions to come to an OBOR/BRI-related agreement. The US has criticized

OBOR as unsustainable, "too good to be true," and as a definite debt trap, with its latest US critique aimed at a likely Italian agreement which would be the first G7 nation to join OBOR/BRI. The Chinese official response was swift: "Foreign ministry in Beijing says US stance is 'laughable' after the White House warned Italy's image would suffer abroad if it signed up for the programme." (Lu, 2019) The Italian response to US warning was captured in a headline by Lau (2019): "Italian PM Giuseppe Conte ignores US warnings and pushes for closer cooperation with China's belt and road Plan."

But the US and Germany are not the only ones raising concerns about participation in OBOR. Even from within the country, the Italian government is divided about whether to join Xi's Initiative.

While terms of the deal, and levels of enthusiasm from Italy's perspective, had varied through the week of March 4, Italy's Prime Minister, Giuseppe Conte declared that BRI cooperation could be "good for Italy." (Balmer, 2019) In addition, the Prime Minister assured constituents that Italy would likely not face any repercussions from the United States, and also added that global security concerns related to Chinese technology companies like Huawei are legitimate. (Balmer, 2019) From an Italian perspective, a BRI partnership could be viewed as an opportunity to jumpstart a flailing economy, and it appears the state would like to focus on an export-related BRI partnership with China. Michele Geraci, an Italian economic advisor, said as much to the *Financial Times*: "We want to make sure that 'Made in Italy' products can have more success in terms of export volume to China, which is the fastest-growing market in the world." (Westcott, 2019)

The situation in Italy will be one worth monitoring. When its BRI partnership comes to fruition, Italy would represent the most developed and "westernized" state to formally sign an agreement with China. However, as many Western powers are harsh critics of BRI policies, the stage could be set for a potential economic policy showdown, and some strong-arming among global powers. In late March, following president Xi's visit, Italy formally announced its agreement to join China's Belt and Road Initiative, becoming the first EU founding member to participate. Grant (2019) remarked on the reaction to the Italian agreement with China. The agreement "set off alarm bells in the White House and groans in the European Union. While the Trump administration fretted about another Chinese attempt to expand its sphere of influence, the EU stressed that Italy was undermining Europe's ability to engage with China as a single bloc."

REFERENCES

 Balmer, C., 2019. "China's Belt and Road plan could be good for Italy: Italian PM." *Reuters* (March 8).

 Girardi, A., 2018. "How China Is Reviving The Silk Road By Buying Ports In The Mediterranean." *Forbes* (December 4).

 Grant, D., 2019. "Italy Should Learn a Thing or Two from Pakistan." *Foreign Policy* (April 1).

 Lau, S., 2019. "Italian PM Giuseppe Conte ignores US warnings and pushes for closer cooperation with China's belt and road plan." *South China Morning Post* (March 12).

 Lu, Z., 2019. "China tells US to mind its own business after Italy is warned not to join Belt and Road Initiative." *South China Morning Post* (March 6).

 Martin, N., 2018. "Report: EU countries to be straitjacketed by China's New Silk Road." DW (April 18).

 OBOReurope, 2018b. "Greece officially joins the BRI." OBOReurope (September 4).

 Oltermann, P., 2018. "Germany's 'China City': how Duisburg became Xi Jinping's gateway to Europe." *The Guardian* (August 1).

 Posaner, J., 2018. "How China put German rust-belt city on the map." *Politico* (January 3).

 Prasad, R., 2018. "EU Ambassadors Condemn China's Belt and Road Initiative." *The Diplomat* (April 21).

Richet, X., 2018. "The 16+1 Format: Chinese presence is fragmented markets on the periphery of Europe." In C. Xin (ed). *16+1 Cooperation and China-EU Relationship*, China-CEE Institute Nonprofit Ltd. Budapest, Hungary (November 20).

 Sheikh, S.R., 2018. "Europe's concerns grow over China's Belt & Road." *Asia Dialogue* (February 15).

 Westcott, B., 2019. "Italy may become largest economy yet to back China's Belt and Road: reports." *CNN* (March 6).

 Xin, C., 2018. *16+1 Cooperation and China-EU Relationship*. China-CEE Institute Nonprofit Ltd. Budapest, Hungary (November 20).

A Great Game in sub-Saharan Africa

China's modern interest in Africa has existed for decades, as exemplified by its support in the continent's struggle against European colonization and for political independence in the 1950s-70s. It then engaged in post-colonial reconstruction and development assistance. China supported Africans, for example, by providing soft diplomacy educational scholarships and financial support for infrastructure projects. One early notable success was the construction of the Tanzania-Zambia (TanZam) railroad, connecting landlocked Zambia to the port of Dar es Salam. This project linked "Zambia's copper belt with the Tanzanian coast 1,100 miles away." (Global Security, 2018) The relationship between sub-Saharan African countries and China has become increasingly strengthened, since the collapse of the Soviet Union and end of the Cold War in the early 1990s.

Contemporary Africa-China cooperation was formalized through the creation of the Forum on China Africa Cooperation (FOCAC) in 2000. (Obera, 2017)

China-Africa relations will be important to monitor over the next few years, as the Belt and Road Initiative continues to evolve; in September 2018, roughly 30+ African leaders attended the China-African Forum on Cooperation summit in Beijing.

Senkpeni (2017) reported a South African deputy minister's remarks to a recent FOCAC meeting:

> FOCAC, consisting of China, the 53 African member states, and the commission of the AU (Africa Union), has become a premium multilateral forum with an impressive record and an ambitious future …. It is truly a shiny example of South-South cooperation.

FOCAC meetings are held every three years and have historically led to further Chinese loans for African states. (Shepherd, 2018)

In mid-2017 Standard Bank researcher Stevens (2017) suggested, "putting it plainly OBOR is the new spearhead for China's foreign policy for the next five to ten years, usurping all other initiatives such as FOCAC and BRICS."

China's OBOR/BRI Initiative has been engaged in developing an accelerated expansion of Chinese investment in sub-Saharan Africa. The cumulative price tag for OBOR/BRI infrastructure-related projects is measured at least in the tens of billions of US dollars. As Simons (2018) reported, "Chinese dealmakers have developed a truly elaborate and sophisticated matrix of engagement archetypes that capture everything from mere 'letter of intent' to ironclad project loan agreements." It is important to note that the amount of funding actually given often proves to be but a fraction of loan amounts being mentioned in press releases.

However, before OBOR was launched in 2013, Sino-African trade and other economic relationships had been on the rise with, for example, Chinese companies bidding for the construction of power plants, roads and railways, as well as mining, including copper, oil and rare minerals. They also won project implementation support from the World Bank and other multilateral development institutions. OBOR is another phase of enhancing the economic and trade relations between Africa and China. For example, by 2015, China-Africa trade had tripled and reached $188 billion USD, surpassing the United States and other countries. (McKinsey and Company, 2017, p. 22)

OBOR/BRI originally targeted Ethiopia, Djibouti and Kenya. Djibouti recently opened a China-built international free trade zone in July 2018. When completed, this free trade zone will be the largest of its kind on the continent, according to Crabtree (2018). China also constructed the deep-water Doraleh Multipurpose Port in Djibouti and has an arrangement to secure a port for a Chinese military naval base there. (Economy, 2018)

Michael H. Glantz

In general, China supplies the expertise, industrial products and labor for its projects and, as a result, these countries have benefited from infrastructure and transportation-related activities. Moreover, similar projects are coming to other parts of Africa including Cameroon, Namibia and Nigeria. (Reboredo, 2017)

China believes that transportation is the founding priority of the success of the BRI in participating countries. (*Xinhua*, 2017a) Its commitment by 2015 to African infrastructure was $21 billion USD. (McKinsey and Company, p. 23) Tarrosy and Vörös (2018) highlighted two recently completed projects in Ethiopia:

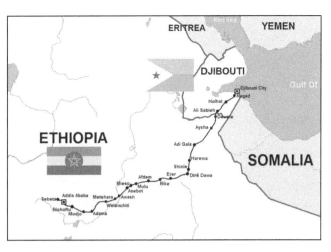

Fig. 34   The rail line from Addis Ababa (Ethiopia) to Djibouti and access to the Indian Ocean. *Skilla 1st, Wikipedia.*

…the first modern light railway (tram) system of sub-Saharan Africa in the capital, Addis Ababa, and the Addis-Djibouti railway, connecting landlocked Ethiopia to the maritime trade routes of the Gulf of Aden and the Red Sea.

The Export-Import Bank of China (Exim Bank) provided concessional loans in the amount of $475 million USD to build the Addis Ababa light rail project. The electric railroad cost $4 billion USD and was implemented by Chinese companies. (Economy, 2018)

"The Export-Import Bank of China [has also] funded a $300 million USD water pipeline system that will transport drinking water from Ethiopia to Djibouti." (Economy, 2018)

In Kenya, a Chinese firm built a new rail line connecting Nairobi to the port city of Mombasa. Obera (2017) reported that "The standard gauge railway and the first three berths at the coastal Lamu Port in Kenya" are other prime examples that are the result of China-Africa cooperation.

China has demonstrated interest in West Africa, as witnessed by the July 2018 state visit to Senegal by President Xi during his first trip to this part of the African continent. Tremann (2018) noted, "In so many ways, Senegal is an ideal partner as China seeks to expand its political and economic reach in Africa." She suggested the following four reasons for Xi's interest in this particular African

country: Senegal has been a strong trading partner with China; it has been economically and politically stable; it is a gateway to the broader West African region; and it has allowed China to create a special economic zone outside of Dakar to access all of western Africa.

Tremann also reported on various West African activities including, but not limited to, a trans-African highway running from Dakar to Djibouti; rehabilitation of the Dakar-Bamako (Mali) rail, a railway link from land-locked Mali to coastal Conakry (Guinea), and major dams in Guinea and the Ivory Coast, among other regional infrastructure activities. China has also provided funds to security forces in the Cameroon to counter jihadist and separatist groups in its northern region.

The expansion of manufacturing activities in Africa is yet another Chinese interest and objective. Examples of China's industrial parks are in Senegal and Ethiopia. Several US companies, including Calvin Klein, have set up shop in a new Hawassa Industrial Park in Ethiopia. (Davison, 2018)

There is growing controversy, however, about China's political, as well as economic, intentions with regard to its infrastructure-related loans and other activities on the continent. Africa is the poorest continent with a population of 1.2 billion in 2017. Sub-Saharan African countries are in dire need of infrastructure in order to develop their economies and China has been providing that infrastructure through loans. However, concerns have been voiced about whether African countries really have the capability to repay those loans.

An Indian newspaper, *The Economic Times* (*ET Online*, 2017), presented a troubling picture of OBOR partnerships in South Asia and has also referred to China's involvement in Africa:

China's strategy to grab land and assets in smaller, less-developed countries is simple: it gives them loans on high rates for infrastructural projects, gets equity into projects, and when the country is unable to repay the loan, it gets ownership of the project. Expect this scenario to unfold in dozens of small countries in Asia and Africa if OBOR projects become the reality. Touted as a global partnership by China, OBOR is actually an exploitative, colonial stratagem to gain vital assets in small countries.

Despite concerns about the ability of African countries to repay their Chinese loans, "data in the field is patchy, at best, and often inaccurate," according to McKinsey and Company. (2017, p. 18) China does not have "a central aid agency and its unique definition of aid…make comparisons with other countries' aid flows difficult."

The contributions of OBOR/BRI, by catalyzing African economic transformation, have revitalized decaying infrastructure and built new ones. It brought China-Africa trade to new levels. The availability of Chinese loans to fund the African projects is playing key roles in economic growth.

China-Africa cooperation is not just symbolic but has been transformative. African optimism is based on the fact that three decades ago China's economy was like that of many African countries today. Africans hope that, through continued collaboration with the Chinese government, their corporations and their people-to-people interactions will follow the Chinese development model.

The Times Group (2017) reported that:

In the West, China's investment into Africa has often been painted in the light of neo-colonialism or of exploitation. China's involvement is also clearly defined by its own interests, not altruism. However, what this criticism fails to address is how China has become so successful in Africa.

China's military activities in Africa merit attention. It provides funds as well as troops for UN Blue Helmet operations in Africa and is now the second largest contributor to the UN peacekeeping budget.

Fisher (2018) reported that "the announcement [in mid-2018] of the China Africa Defense and Security Forum (CADSF) is unprecedented and came without warning." He noted its creation was apparently favored by most African countries.

Fig. 35 Are African countries painting themselves into a proverbial corner with no excape from debt traps? *V. Ndula.*

Fisher went on to note that "despite this level of military engagement with Africa through existing organizations, Beijing decided that it required its own China-centric, pan-African defense organization." Apparently, this is the PLA's contribution to China's "going out" policy. Interestingly, Fisher quoted "the Director of the China Association of International Studies, commenting on CADSF…that China may seek a base on the West coast of Africa."

Kovrig (2018) reported "This rising role in security undergirds Beijing's economic statecraft and commercial interest in Africa, helps professionalize China's military and protects its citizens there, and furthers its ambitions to be a major power with global influence." China's various bilateral and multilateral military affairs in Africa have sharply increased since the OBOR Initiative was launched in 2013.

In addition to the increasing role of the Chinese military in sub-Saharan Africa, there has been an increase in the use of China's private security companies. As reported by Legarda and Nouwens (2018):

Following the build-up of infrastructure and investment projects along China's extensive Belt and Road Initiative (BRI), private security companies from China are also increasingly going global – to protect Chinese assets and the growing number of Chinese nationals living and working in countries along the BRI, in sometimes unstable regions.

One Belt One Road: A Debt Trap or a Positive Force for African Development?

Since the original OBOR Initiative has expanded from its inception in 2013, some observers question if the massive loans and infrastructure investments are truly beneficial to developing nations in general and to African countries specifically. While supporters have argued that Chinese infrastructure investments constitute a boon to the general African economy, critical parties, such as India and the United States, accuse the Chinese initiative of burdening impoverished nations with massive amounts of debt.

On August 28, China's Vice Commerce Minister Qian Keming deflected claims that Africa's debt can be traced to BRI:

> When it comes to the debt problem, there really is not that much Chinese debt in Africa.... Overall, according to the statistics that I have, the majority of the debt burden is not necessarily created by China. (Shepherd, 2018)

His comments highlight a conflicting understanding between the larger Western world and China about BRI's impact in developing states. China insists that their initiative-related loans are not debt traps or, worse, not part of "debt-trap diplomacy," while critics point to the mounting debts for states which were already in difficult fiscal shape. One measure of the health of a country's economy is the debt-to-GDP ratio which for Djibouti is estimated to be above an untenable 90%, meaning it is impossible to repay its loans to China. The ratio for Kenya is estimated at above 50% which raises a red flag for its ability to repay its loan installments to China. In his article entitled "China to Take Over Kenya's Largest Port Over Unpaid Chinese Loan," Durden (2018) offered the following observation:

> After years of "benevolent" handouts to various African countries by Beijing, all of which however came in the form of loans, of which few have led to viable, long-term projects and cash-flow generating assets, and led to accusations that China is pursuing a "new colonialism" of the continent (and more recently along the One Belt One Road corridor), China is demonstrating to the world what happens when its debtors refuse to pay up.

There is a new crack in the OBOR/BRI non-disclosure with Kenya. Rudolph (2019) summarized the Kenyan *Daily Nation*'s mid-January 2019 exposure to the world of the 2011 Kenya agreement for Chinese loans to develop its infrastructure. The exposure shines light onto the wording of such agreements with other countries, wording that has been tagged as extremely troublesome for the borrower. If true, Kenya's agreement provides insight into claims about a predatory Chinese process of debt-trap diplomacy. Concern about debt traps became heightened when Sri Lanka's Hambantota deep-water port fell under China's control with a 99-year lease, following the country's inability to repay its loan. The following few points expose a few of Kenya's debt trap risks:

- Kenya's national assets are offered as collateral in case loan obligations cannot be met.
- No outside funds can be used to repay the loan without permission from China.
- All disputes arising about the loans are to be arbitrated in China and by Chinese authorities.

If Kenyan loan payments were to be in default, Kenya would become China's neo-colony in Africa.

China has recently introduced the concept of "sustainable" African debt. Hong Kong's *South China Morning Post* quoted Qian Keming explaining, "As the next step, we will discuss with African countries about how to promote a sustainable model for debt." (Wong, 2018) As defined in *Wikipedia* (2019), "Sustainable debt is the level of debt which allows a debtor country to meet its current and future debt service obligations in full, without recourse to further debt relief or rescheduling, avoiding accumulation of arrears, while allowing an acceptable level of economic growth."

While a concept of "sustainable debt" makes an interesting media "sound bite," it remains to be seen which conditions and concessions Chinese leadership plans to enact in order to make massive BRI-related debts remotely close to being sustainable. Furthermore, Chinese claims that it is not the largest cause of African debt, a statement that will likely "creep" toward inaccuracy with each major "investment" that China makes in Africa. What might have begun as China's desire to secure raw materials for its factories has turned into an opportunity to become deeply involved in continent-wide political, economic and security affairs.

Fig. 36　Chinese rail bridge construction technology at work in Africa. *P. E.O. Usher.*

REFERENCES

 Crabtree, J., 2018. "While China slaps tariffs on the US, it's also championing free trade in Africa." *CNBC* (July).

 Davison. W., 2018. "Industrial Parks Are Africa's Latest Gamble to Lure Chinese Manufacturers." *China File* (January 3).

 Durden, T., 2018. "China To Take Over Kenya's Largest Port Over Unpaid Chinese Loan." Zero Hedge (Dec 27).

 ET Online, 2017. "China's dream of global dominance is cracking at early stages." *The Economic Times* (November 17).

 Economy, E.C., 2018. "China's Strategy in Djibouti: Mixing Commercial and Military Interests." Council on Foreign Relations (April 13).

 Fisher Jr., R.D., 2018. "China Militarizes Its Influence in Africa." *The National Interest* (November 25).

 Global Security, 2018. "Tanzania – TANZAM Railway." Global Security (n.d.)

 Kovrig, M., 2018. "China's expanding military footprint in Africa." *Mail & Guardian* (October 24).

 McKinsey and Company, 2017. "Dance of the lions and dragons: How are Africa and China engaging, and how will the partnership evolve?" *Africa Newsroom* (June).

 Obera, F., 2017. "Africa to benefit from China's $124 billion plan for "One Belt, One Road" project." *This Is Africa* (May).

 Reboredo, R., 2017. "Why China's audacious building plans could be a major strain on African economies." *The Conversation* (September).

 Rudolph, J., 2019. "Chinese Loan to Kenya Stokes BRI Concerns." *China Digital Times* (January 16).

 Senkpeni, A. D., 2017. "Beijing Officials Meeting Sets Tone For 2018 China-Africa Cooperation Summit". *Front Page Africa* (November 26).

 Shepherd, C., 2018. "China says projects not to blame for majority of Africa debt." *Reuters* (August 28).

 Simons, B., 2018. "China is generous in promising billions to Africa but is tough in redeeming pledges." *Quartz Africa* (September 3).

 Stevens, J., 2017. "One Belt One Road (OBOR) and Africa." Tralac (June 2).

 Tarrosy, I. and Z. Vörös, 2018. "China and Ethiopia, Part 1: The Light Railway System." *The Diplomat* (February).

 The Times Group, 2017. "Will Africa Benefit from Chinas OBOR Initiative?" *Times Group Malawi* (November 7).

 Tremann, C., 2018. "Xi Jinping, Senegal, and China's West Africa Drive." Lowy Institute (July 20).

 Wikipedia, 2018. "External Debt." (February 5).

 Wong, C., 2018. "China aims for 'sustainable' debt with Africa as Belt and Road Initiative comes under fire from West." *South China Morning Post* (August 28).

 Xinhua, 2017a. "China signs over 130 transport pacts with Belt and Road countries." *China Daily* (April 20).

A Functional Space Silk Road:
The Belt and Road Goes 3-D

The idea for creating a silk road in space was proposed in 2014, the year following the launching of OBOR. China's existing space program was a new aspect of the family of geographic roads and belts. According to Assef (2018), its initial goal was "to control the high ground of space from Asia to Europe via a satellite constellation configuration," a constellation being a set of satellites that communicate with each other. "Most navigation services in the world use signals from GPS, which is owned by the US Government, and operated by the US Airforce." (Zhou, 2018)

The objective of the Space Silk Road is ostensibly to supply communications to China's BRI partners in Eurasia, Africa and the Middle East for industry, transport, natural hazard and disaster warning, and earth observations related to sea level rise, melting polar ice, and atmospheric changes, along with other information services. Such systems in space will be used as well to support routine military objectives and in wartime if the need were to arise. Clearly, a satellite navigation system has a wide range of national security applications.

Viewing China's space effort as an additional silk road energized those Chinese industries involved in the country's space program as well as in smart technology manufacturing to think of broader applications. It has also been referred to as "the Belt & Road Initiative Space Information Corridor." The Space Silk Road has geopolitical implications as well as implications for research, communication and monitoring.

China has been creating its own independent satellite constellation to serve the BRI community (the Bei-Dou Navigation Satellite System [BDS]) with BeiDou-3 and its proposed 35 satellites by 2020. "Beidou is one of the only four global navigation networks along with GPS, Russia's GLONASS and the European space agency's Galileo." (Zhou, 2018) It can be viewed in part as a "direct

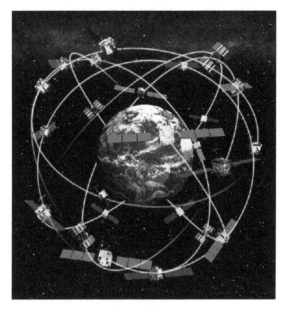

Fig. 37   China's satellite aspirations will serve both civilian and military goals. *NOAA, Wikipedia.*

response to the US ambitions in the Pacific that were ensconced within the Trans Pacific Partnership." (Assef, 2018) Zhou (2018) noted that "China has spent years developing its own 'homegrown' navigation system to rival [the US's] GPS as it seeks to reduce its reliance on foreign technology. This [Christmas] week, the Chinese government announced that its satellite navigation system...has achieved global coverage."

Assef also suggested that "not only will the Space Silk Road deliver significant commercial opportunities for China and for Chinese companies, but it will also support the collaborative, expansionary foreign policy that President Xi Jinping is championing as a key benefit delivered by BRI." (p. 2)

As of today, the BRI region encompasses scores of countries with a cumulative population in excess of two billion people. Australian writer Davis (2017) succinctly summarized the emerging East-West showdown in space that is likely to occur in the next decade:

Space competition can be seen as an extension of terrestrial geopolitics and control of the high ground of space allows domination of earth because if information is the basis of 21st Century power, space is the domain through which that information will flow. A Chinese Space Silk Road would add a new layer of Chinese power and control over much of Eurasia and, unchallenged, would lock out Western companies and ensure Beijing was the sole provider of space services to BRI states. That would ultimately lock in Chinese control of BRI economies."

As countries in Latin America and other regions in Africa besides East Africa, for example, become more engaged with Chinese infrastructure development partnerships, China's influence over them from space would surely increase. China's influence would then be truly global. Davis warned the West, "That's never going to be a good outcome for the US in its broader competition with China for strategic primacy in Asia."

The US-China Economic and Security Review Commission issued a report in early January (Wilson, 2017) on "China's Alternative to GPS and its Implications for the United States." Just as GPS was originally driven by military objectives, "China made the determination to develop Beidou based on its security requirements." China's Beidou Navigation Satellite System (BDS) had been in development for the past 25 years. As a result, "Since 1994 China has spent billions of dollars to develop a product that is already free: satellite navigation services provided globally by the US Global Positioning System (GPS)." "China has stated that it plans to expand Beidou coverage to most of the countries covered in its 'One Belt One Road' Initiative by 2018 on the way to global coverage in 2020." It has made considerable headway toward achieving its 2020 operational goals. (Wilson, 2017)

An interesting reason for developing a BDS independent of GPS was suggested by Wilson (2017, p.6):

The PLA [People's Liberation Army] has considered [its] dependence on a foreign PNT [positioning, navigation and timing information] system to be a strategic vulnerability since at least the mid-1980s. These fears were exacerbated during the 1995-1996 Taiwan Straits Crisis. According to a retired PLA general, the PLA concluded that an unexpected disruption to GPS caused the PLA to lose track of some of the ballistic missiles it fired into the Taiwan Strait during the crisis. He then said that "it was a great shame for the PLA…an unforgettable humiliation. That's how we made up our mind to develop our own global [satellite] navigation and positioning system, no matter how huge the cost. Beidou is a must for us. We learned it the hard way."

Beijing's decision to develop the Beidou System as an alternative to GPS will surely have security, military, economic, and diplomatic consequences for Chinese relations with the United States. The development of the Beidou System also fulfills a highly-desired objective of President Xi, the integrating of military and civilian affairs.

As China nears its goal of providing satellite navigation coverage by 2020 and growing numbers of Beidou-configured products enter the vast downstream market…state-affiliated customers in China will probably avoid US technologies once China's industry becomes mature.

The US, specifically, and Western countries in general are now very concerned about China's accelerating activities to construct an independent satellite constellation-based BDS and its space-related activities.

REFERENCES

 Assef, N., 2018. "China's Control of the Heavens: An Overview of the Rapidly Developing Space Silk Road." SSRN (May 9).

 Davis, M., 2017. "The Coming of China's Space Silk Road." *The Strategist*. ASPI (Australian Strategic Policy Institute) (August 11).

 Wilson, J., 2017. "China's Alternative to GPS and its Implications for the United States." Staff Report of the U.S.-China Economic and Security Review Commission (January 5). pp. 2, 3, 7, 8.

 Zhou, V., 2018. "China's answer to GPS now covers the entire world." *Ink stone News* (Dec 28).

A Digital Silk Road

A "digital silk road" is based on information and communication technologies (ICTs). It is another "functional" silk road that will provide information electronically to Belt and Road countries in Asia, Europe, Africa, and wherever else China arranges to operate. The Space Silk Road satellite infrastructure will enable the monitoring from space of environmental and other changes on the surface of the globe. Such information can be used in support of smart cities in the effective and efficient management of urban environments such as water use, traffic circulation, and even the planning of urban sprawl. Several of the countries in the OBOR/BRI geographic and functional spheres of influence could benefit from such information and communication technology-driven services.

Brown (2017) noted "The idea of incorporating digital sectors like telecommunications, internet-of-things infrastructure, and e-commerce into One Belt One Road (OBOR) is not new. The March 2015 white paper articulating the vision for OBOR called for growth in digital trade and the expansion of communications networks to develop 'an information silk road'."

There are several sustainable development objectives that can be addressed successfully by an effective space program. The streams of information gathered by China's Space Silk Road's satellite constellation would be a digital belt and road (DBAR, 2017), providing environmental observations, imagery and monitoring of land and sea to countries participating in OBOR/BRI's ecosystem. Huadong (2018) noted that "sharing big data from satellite imagery and other Earth observations across Asia, the Middle East and east Africa is key to sustainability." He identified a range of space-derived big data sets to be shared with BRI countries, noting key decision-making challenges such as "adapting to climate and environmental change, mitigating disaster risk, managing water supply, increasing agriculture and food security, protecting natural and cultural heritage, sustainable development of urban areas and infrastructure, managing coast and marine areas, and understanding changes in high mountains and the Arctic."

At the 2017, Fourth World Internet Conference in Wuzhen, China, it became clear that a digital silk road had a strong geopolitical underpinning. "Cybertechnology leaders and government officials from around the world gathered…to discuss the future of the global digital economy." Besides being of great value for internal development in China, it has the potential for tremendous influence globally. Viney et al. (2017) noted:

> As President Xi Jinping reiterated during his opening statement…. China's cyberspace channels are "entering a fast lane [and] will become more and more open." This comment was a response to complaints from Western cyber-tech corporations such as Google, Facebook and Apple about Chinese censorship. Xi made clear that "cyber sovereignty" will most definitely remain a key part of China's vision of global internet expansion.

China is striving to free itself in the next several years from its dependence on the US and the West's worldwide dominance of the internet highway. Former French Prime Minister, Villepin, attending the Wuzhen conference, observed "There has been a technological shift from the West to the East with the rise of internet champions in China as an alternative to the US monopoly." (quoted in Viney et al., 2017)

REFERENCES

 Brown, R., 2017. "Beijing's Silk Road Goes Digital." Council on Foreign Relations (June 6).

 DBAR, 2017. "Digital Belt and Road Program Science Plan Release." Digital Belt and Road (December 3).

 Huadong, G., 2018. "Steps to the digital Silk Road." *Nature*, Comments. 554, 25-27 (January 30).

 Viney, S., N. Pan and J. Fang, (2017). "One Belt, One Road: China heralds 'Digital Silk Road'; foresees internet-era power shift soon." *ABC (Australia)* (December 5).

Sea Ports as a Functional Silk Road

Chinese involvement in port construction as part of its broader OBOR/BRI vision started out in a stealth-like fashion by refurbishing a port here and a port there. One critical perspective about China's Belt and Road Initiative commented on this stealth-like approach of China with regard to ports in a Greater Europe. Lee (2018) suggested in an article provocatively titled "China's Trojan Ports" that "China is now applying its well-tested South China Sea approach – gradually asserting *de facto* control and dominance through incremental actions, each of which will not provoke a robust counter response – in Europe.… However, unlike in the South China Sea, Chinese economic and investment policies toward Europe are not militarily threatening."

Lee also noted that, as of today:

> It is estimated that state-backed Chinese investors own at least 10 percent of all equity in ports in Europe, with deals inked in Greece, Spain, Italy, France, the Netherlands and Belgium. This is in addition to a growing investment portfolio of at least 40 ports in North and South America, Africa, the Middle East, Eastern Europe, Central Asia, South and Southeast Asia, Australia and the Pacific.

Fig. 38 Idealized watercolor of a deep-sea port and cargo ship. *CCB.*

The Greek port of Piraeus serves as an interesting example of China's port projects abroad. Singh (2018) highlighted it in the following way:

> In Greece, COSCO, a Chinese state-owned enterprise acquired a 67 percent stake in the Greek container port of Piraeus, along China's One Belt (OBOR) project. Piraeus is an entry point into Europe and helps connect the maritime route of the OBOR with the main sea routes through the Indian Ocean region to Europe. In addition, China also acquired a 51 percent stake in Greece's public power grid operator.

Singh then suggested how this risky economic venture actually turned into a soft-power win for China. He observed that "In June 2017, Greece stunned the world and paid 'political interest' to China by vetoing an EU resolution at the UN condemning China's Human Rights record."

Other ports, such as Djibouti's Doraleh Port, Sri Lanka's port of Hambantota, and Pakistan's Gwadar, each have their own interesting stories. However, it is now obvious that China's interest in ports, especially deep-water ones, has become a strategic goal in an economic, political and military sense. "While China's new array of port holdings [terminals, port operations, cargo ships], are fundamentally economically motivated projects there is a glaring political dimension," noted Shepard (2017a). He continued:

> It seems as if it is now almost daily news to hear about how a Chinese state-owned shipping firm has purchased a seaport or won the rights to develop a new ocean or land terminal in another country.… These new acquisitions add to China's growing portfolio of international holdings, which now span the world.

OBOR/BRI is truly an ambitious program for several reasons: First, it is China's attempt to create regional trade arrangements and a new China-centric world order for the 21st Century. A new world order would mean there would no longer be a global economic power dominated by the West, which has been the case for the few decades following the collapse of the Soviet Union and the end of the Cold War in the early 1990s. China has proposed to use upwards of $4 trillion USD to support infrastructure worldwide, mainly to help developing countries realize their economic development potential in a way that would also make them partners in China's activities. By focusing on infrastructure, the Chinese Government and state-owned enterprises would operate along the new silk routes in scores of OBOR/BRI-participating countries in dire need of modernized infrastructure. Financial assistance to them would meet their various development needs and wants while at the same time enabling China to use its surplus manufacturing capacity and ageing workforce to produce and provide the materials and expertise necessary for infrastructure construction.

A benefit to China of its soft power is the building of longer-term relationships with present and next generations in countries in Central, South, Southwest, West and Southeast Asia. People-to-people programs, for example, provide Chinese languages courses for students and professionals in OBOR/BRI partnering countries and provide cultural exchanges with them as well. This creates a positive view of China to inhabitants and governments of OBOR/BRI partnering countries. To this end, Xi'an Jiaotong University in mid-2015, formed the University Alliance of the Silk Road (UASR) involving 132 universities from 32 OBOR-related countries. People-to-people exchanges with Kazakhstan, a key China partner in OBOR, has received special attention. (HKPU, 2016)

Although the Belt and Road effort is expected to take decades to carry out (2049 is its official end date), China stands to gain new trade partners and to secure access to natural resources along the way, as well as access to new markets for its goods and services. It is an apparent "win-win" situation from China's perspective…a win for China, a win for its OBOR/BRI partners.

An article by *Port Technology* (2018) entitled "China's Top Three Belt and Road Initiatives," identified the following three OBOR/BRI ports of great importance: Singapore, Djibouti and, surprisingly, Duisberg (Germany).

Why Singapore?

China has invested more in Singapore than it has in any other BRI country. About two thirds of China's Outward Direct Investment (ODI) goes to Singapore.

Why Djibouti?

This port is "located on the tip of the Horn of Africa. It is a gateway to the Red Sea and on the path between Europe and Asia." "As much as 20 percent of global trade passes [through the Bab-el-Mandeb Strait] between Yemen and the Port of Djibouti." [Djibouti owes more than 80 percent of its foreign debt to China.] (Dorsey, 2018) Djibouti is also the home of China's first overseas military base.

Why Duisberg?

As home of the world's largest inland port, this German city is an extremely important part of the BRI…. With its prime location at the end of the Chongqing-Xinjiang-Europe rail-line, which opened in 2011, Duisberg receives up to 25 freight convoys from China's big electronic hubs every week with each trip taking just 13 days…. From Duisberg, the products have access to the Rhine and the North Sea.

Had we picked three important ports, they would have been Piraeus (Greece), Djibouti, Gwadar (Pakistan); a fourth choice would have been Hambantota (Sri Lanka).

Piraeus – Among those initiatives, China plans to make the Greek port of Piraeus the "dragon head" of its vast "One Belt One Road" project, a new Silk Road into Europe. (Horowitz and Alderman, 2017)

Djibouti – China now controls the deepwater port of Djibouti. It has built its first military base outside China there, in a strategic location at the southern end of the Red Sea across from war-torn Yemen.

Gwadar – Gwadar is a an OBOR/BRI major Arabian Sea port in Pakistan that will be at the end of transportation routes passing through Kashmir, a region over which India claims sovereignty. It is central to China's plan to provide access for Xinjiang to a sea port. The pipeline will enable the flow of crude oil to China's landlocked Xinjiang. However, Gwadar is in Pakistan's Baluchistan province, a regional hotspot, as Baluchis seek autonomy, if not independence, from Pakistan.

Michael H. Glantz

Hambantota – This deep-water port was taken over by China because Sri Lanka could not re-pay its loans. It has become the symbol of a debt trap to potential and existing BRI partner countries that take loans from China in order to pay for infrastructure.

**News Flash
The Darwin Port Dilemma
(Australia)**

In October 2015, Australia's Northern Territory (NT) government voluntarily leased its port of Darwin for 99 years to a Chinese company with alleged strong ties to the Chinese Government. The NT granted 80 percent control of the port and nearby coastal land to China. (Clifford, 2017) The Obama Administration was blindsided, learning about the done deal after the fact. Smee and Walsh (2016) in their article "How the sale of Darwin port to the Chinese sparked a geopolitical brawl" observed that "The US and China had been shadowboxing in the South China Sea and the port of Darwin was the southern flank of the US operations in the Pacific." The leasing to China was viewed by the US as a weakening of the American presence and military activities in the greater Southeast Asian region.

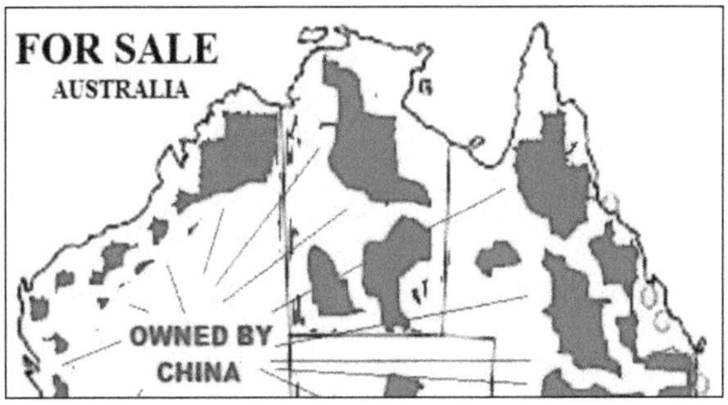

Garrick (2018) recently noted: "But now, by design or not, the Darwin port deal increasingly looks like a blueprint for how Chinese interests can take control of foreign ports – as it is doing around the world – without arousing local opposition." He went on to note that at the time "All levels of Australian government have encouraged it…. In fact, Infrastructure Australia advised privatization of the port."

Garrick suggested that "Darwin is now unwittingly on the front line in managing tensions between Australia's most important strategic ally and partner [the US] and its major trading partner [China]." Ever since the lease was arranged, the Australian Government has been criticized over Chinese direct investments in the country. The government has since then tightened laws on direct and indirect foreign investments. Several articles appeared in Australian media, commenting about both pros and cons of the strategic impacts of the leasing of its furthest-north deep-water port.

The Australia Defence Association (ADA, 2015) headlined its strategic review of the leasing with "The

Fig. 39 "Stop selling Australia over seas. Reform our foreign ownership policy." *Care2 Petition.*

Botched 99-year lease of Darwin's commercial port shows grand-strategic failures in national decision-making."

Preserving an appropriate degree of long-term national control over such key strategic infrastructure necessarily overrides any short-term and sectional interests locally, especially when they arise from only parochially-focused political expediency…. In geostrategic terms, Darwin harbor and its city provide the only location suitable for major naval use across northern Australia should this ever be necessary.

While political leaders in the Northern Territory appear to exhibit few, if any, regrets about this 99-year lease, the Australian Government has continued to show seller's remorse. Although Australia is not part of ASEAN's Southeast Asia, one might consider it an emerging part "Greater Southeast Asia" that is slowly expanding the Chinese regional sphere of influence.

**New Flash
BRI in Peru: COSCO's First South American Deep-Water Port**

Recent articles expose the depth of actual and proposed involvement of Chinese corporations in Peru. China has invested in energy, mining, telecommunications, construction and financing. (Harashima, 2019) COSCO "now operates 52 ports and terminals around the world, and is expected to continue its expansion," including such ports as Piraeus, Rotterdam and Abu Dhabi. It is developing a major terminal at the port at Chancay on the Peruvian coast north of Lima. Zhong (2019) wrote about the importance of COSCO's first port in South America:

It is a natural deep-water harbor with a maximum of 16-meter water depth and is capable of meeting the needs of mega vessels. The construction of Chancay terminal includes multipurpose terminals, container terminals and related infrastructure facilities. Phase one of the terminal will have four berths, of which two are multipurpose berths, and two are container berths….

China is already heavily invested in Peruvian mines with projects to develop rail lines to Peruvian ports that would allow for exports from Bolivia, Brazil and other trade partners. China is also likely to develop another deep-water port at Ilo, a copper mining region, in southern Peru. The Peruvian government has embraced the BRI as a major source of investment, ignoring recent US secretaries of state's warnings to be wary of such development loan arrangements with China and involvement in OBOR/BRI.

REFERENCES

 Dorsey, J.M., 2018. "Pakistan's financial crisis puts OBOR in jeopardy." *Global Village Space* (July 7).

 Harashima, D., 2019. "Cosco's Peru port buy latest in China's Belt and Road push." *Nikkei Asian Review* (February 15).

 HKPU, 2016. "International Forum: Nurturing Talent and Building Capacity in Supporting the Belt and Road Development." Hong Kong Polytechnic University (May).

 Horowitz J. and L. Alderman, 2017. "Chastised by E.U., a Resentful Greece Embraces China's Cash and Interests." *New York Times* (August 26).

 Lee, J., 2018. "China's Trojan Ports." *The American Interest* (November 29).

 Port Technology, 2018. "China's Top Three Belt and Road Initiatives." *Port Technology* (July 24).

 Shepard, W., 2017a. "China's Seaport Shopping Spree: What China Is Winning By Buying Up The World's Ports." *Forbes* (September 6).

 Singh, M., 2018. "From Smart Power to Sharp Power: How China Promotes her National Interests." *Journal of Defense Studies (India)*, Vol. 12, No. 3 (July-September) pp. 5-25.

 Zhong N., 2018. "Chinese company buys 60% stake in Peru port." *China Daily* (January 28).

China's Silk Road in the Air

Airports appear in the OBOR/BRI listing of projects along with oil and gas pipelines, highways, roads, railroads, ports, energy grids, communications, space and digital silk roads. However, most of the emphasis appears to have been placed on discussing in detail each of the above, with the exception of airports. China has embarked on linking its cities with the other ports: foreign airports. In fact, the Air Silk Road had become an initiative-in-the-making a year or so following the first announcement of OBOR.

China's *Go Abroad* (2016) reported that reforms of the Civil Aviation Administration of China (CAAC) had in 2015 "proposed to further open up airspace, optimize the allocation of international traffic rights and encourage [the country's] civil aviation enterprises to 'go out' and compete in the international aviation market through the use of capital." Unless one searches specifically for information about a China's air or aerial silk road, it is difficult to find it in popular articles. It is much less in the news than are deep-water ports situated along the world's oceans.

An Air Silk Road requires upgrading of many of China's domestic airports, increasing the number of international routes, increasing the capacity and expansion of international routes, opening up airspace for flight routes to and from OBOR/BRI countries, increasing enterprise strength, increasing agreements with foreign companies, and enhancing domestic aviation manufacturing.

Go Abroad (2016) also observed:

By acquiring (or investing in) a number of foreign airports (Parchim International Airport in Germany, Heathrow Airport in the UK, Parma Airport in Italy, Toulouse-Blagnac Airport in France, and Tirana International Airport in Albania), Chinese enterprises have seized the opportunity from the market downturn [in 2008] and expanded in the international aviation market.

There are many other foreign airports that China has invested in, such as in Togo, Nepal, the Maldives, Sri Lanka and Zambia. In sum, "The expansion of air routes and the development of air transport are priority areas of the 'One Belt One Road' [BRI]."

Han (2015) noted that "Aviation is set to play an increasingly large role in China's commitment to strengthen the economic capacity and connectivity among the nations within the OBOR area." Not unlike the risks associated with other Chinese infrastructure port project loans, China can eventually take over airport facilities, if loan repayments are delayed or defaulted. Such a prospect was raised, for example, by Krah (2018) who noted: "China is now proposing to take over the Kenneth Kaunda International Airport, should Zambia Government fail to pay back its huge foreign debt on time. The issue of whether Zambia possess[es] the required economic muscle to repay that debt is in contention considering the amount involved. It's typical of the Chinese strategy."

REFERENCES

 Go Abroad, 2016. "Analysis of the 'One Belt, One Road' initiative – Telecommunications and Aviation sectors." 4th issue. EY (September).

 Han, B., 2015. "China's Silk Road Takes to the Air." *The Diplomat* (October 13).

 Krah, R., 2018. "China to take over Zambian international Airport for debt repayment default; neocolonialism?" Committee for the Abolition of Illegitimate Debt (September 1).

OBOR/BRI is not without its Challenges

Some countries have wondered aloud whether OBOR/BRI is just a veiled attempt by China to keep its domestic factories and workers in full operation by using its excess capacity and its workers employed overseas to work on its infrastructure development projects around the globe. Western governments also wonder about China's long-term geopolitical objectives. Still others wonder if China's goal is just to create a counterbalance to the American presence in Asia, the Pacific Rim, in the developing world and in space.

An incident frequently highlighted by India, and commented on by many others, centered on the construction of Sri Lanka's Hambantota deep-water port. It sparked concern about China's long-term strategy. Stacey (2017) wrote in an article, "China signs 99-year lease on Sri Lanka's Hambantota port," that the Sri Lankan government, unable to pay on its $8 billion USD loan from China and, in lieu of debt repayment, agreed to turn over a "70 percent stake in the joint venture" to the Chinese government under a 99-year lease. The take-over of the Sri Lanka port by China is being used by China's opponents, especially India and the US, as a "red flag" warning to potential partners seeking Chinese loans for their infrastructure projects.

Stacey went on to note the likely adverse consequences for China's other OBOR partners:

> Beijing typically finds a local partner, makes that local partner accept investment plans that are detrimental to their country in the long term, and then uses the debts to either acquire the project altogether or to acquire political leverage in that country.… In recent months, however, there have been signs that China's partners are starting to become wary over the terms being dictated to build projects under the One Road banner. Pakistan, Nepal and Myanmar have all recently cancelled or sidelined major hydroelectricity projects planned by Chinese companies. The projects would have been worth a total of $20bn [USD].

Myanmar, too, had been pursuing an agreement with China to develop a deep-water port, as well as a special economic zone in which China would get preferential treatment, at Kyaukpyu on the western coast of the country. It is in the Rakhine state, which has been the site of the Myanmar government's "genocide" of its Muslim Rohingya population. While Western countries have condemned the genocide, China remained silent and non-antagonistic toward the government, because China has pledged not to get involved in an OBOR/BRI partnering nation's internal political controversy.

This port would give China's landlocked Yunnan Province access to Mideast oil via a pipeline across neighboring Myanmar. The original design of the port had ten berths, but was scaled back to two berths with the sharp reduction of Myanmar's loan from and debt to China. The project was scaled back, as suggested in *The Guardian* (2018), because "Myanmar officials said the experience of Sri Lanka, where this year the government signed over to China the lease on a strategic port to pay off Chinese-backed loans used to finance it, had raised concerns the country could be walking into a debt trap."

Perhaps several of the problems facing China can be related to perceptions held by outsiders about what China is doing around the globe. Are those actions of a friend or of a foe? Primiano (2018) explicitly stated the following concern that other countries might secretly harbor about various development-oriented outreach activities:

> Based on the fundamental changes that Xi Jinping has initiated [under the umbrella of] the Asia Infrastructure Investment Bank, the Belt and Road Initiative (BRI), the China Dream, China's island building…for the ostensible purpose of projecting military force in the South China Sea, the crackdown on civil society in China, etc., it is clear that Xi Jinping is determined to advance his version of China's preferences in world politics…. Considering that Xi has advanced a very ambitious agenda in

Michael H. Glantz

Fig. 40   Possible risks associated with OBOR/BRI. *CCB, adapted from Anon.*

just his first five years in office, there is no reason for why we should expect anything less ambitious in the years to come.

There has been an increase in articles questioning China's ability to continue the business-as-usual OBOR/BRI loans it has been making to politically or economically unstable developing countries and enterprises that are at high risk to default on their loans. An interesting risk map in China's *GoAbroad* (2016) exposed the levels of risk for OBOR/BRI project partnering countries for falling into a debt trap.

The potential biases of various observers notwithstanding, there are challenging issues raised about the long-term sustainability of the OBOR/BRI. As the OBOR/BRI matures, questions about its economic viability are increasingly being raised. The issues raised by these questions and concerns should identify lessons that need to be learned both by China (governments, banks and companies) and by prospective OBOR/BRI partners.

Most recently, articles are appearing that question whether such an ambitious global infrastructure development initiative is really viable in the long run. While China can control its actions and what it chooses to invest in to meet a wide range of its objectives, there are intervening factors over which it has little to no control. China's ability to provide loans to developing economies can be reduced by happenings in the global economy, whether a trade war with the US, a downturn in its economy, or an economic inability of people around the globe to buy its goods and services.

One of the most critical opinion pieces recently published was written by political scientist Minxin Pei (2019). Pei observed that "The news for China's ambitious Belt and Road Initiative after five years of OBOR/BRI, has been relatively bad." He commented on recent policy reversals in loan-recipient countries of Pakistan, Myanmar and the Maldives, each of which seeking some sort of redress from the burdensome loan arrangements of their government. As one indicator, Pei noted that the number of *China Daily* articles on BRI was less in 2018 than in 2017. He suggested "If we keep track of BRI stories in the official Chinese media in 2019 and compared the coverage with previous years we should have a clearer picture about where BRI is headed."

Pei noted four key warning signs to support his view: (1) a likely decline in foreign exchange earnings in coming years; (2) rising pension costs of its aging population; (3) slowing economic growth; and (4) dwindling tax revenues. He called it a perfect storm. Pei concluded with the following pessimistic comment on OBOR/BRI's future:

What appears to be happening in Beijing is that while its leaders continue to stand by BRI, Xi's original ambitions [what Pei labelled as BRI 1.0] are being rolled back out of public view. We should not be surprised if Beijing eventually lets BRI, at least BRI 1.0, die quietly.

The pressures on Xi's OBOR/BRI are real and continuing to grow, after five years of experience, as Pei pointed out. Assuming that those pressures cast a shadow on its ability to succeed in the future, China can turn the current crisis into a more favorable, successful and fair future for it and its OBOR/BRI existing partners as well as prospective new ones. Existing loan agreements, for example, can be reviewed, and inequities and other grievances redressed. Future loan MOUs and contracts can be transparent. Both lender and loan recipient would benefit from following more effective agreements with transparency. To be sure, the pressures on China, including those brought on by the US-China trade war, will bring to an end the so-named BRI 1.0, but it would likely be replaced by a new more equitable BRI 2.0 as the next phase of the Chinese Communist Party's "Long March toward 2049" and to China's geopolitical superpower status.

Selected Weblines Question China's Intent

- The new colonialism: China's BRI or silk road project is coming to be seen across Asia as the road to ruin.
- EU Envoys slam China's and Belt and Road Initiative, says it will hit free trade.
- If China doesn't act like private sector, BRI partners may desert Silk Road.
- China's massive 'Belt and Road' spending spree has caused concern around the world, and now its China's turn to worry.
- China's dream of global dominance is cracking at early stages.
- Chinas global dreams give its neighbors nightmares.
- China's BRI may 'swamp weak nations in debt'.
- China's Belt and Road Initiative is falling short.
- China's Belt and Road projects drive overseas debt fears.
- China's BRI is the most ambitious investment effort in history. But is it also a plan to remake the global balance of power?

REFERENCES

 Go Abroad, 2016. "Analysis of the 'One Belt, One Road' initiative – Telecommunications and Aviation sectors." 4th issue. EY (September).

 The Guardian, 2018. "Myanmar scales back Chinese-backed port project over debt fears." *Reuters* (August 2).

 Pei, M., 2019. "Will China let Belt and Road die quietly?" *Nikkei Asian Review* (February 15).

 Primiano, C. B., 2018. "The end of China's term limits and its 'Peaceful Rise'." *Asia Dialogue* (April 26).

 Stacey, K., 2017. "China signs 99-year lease on Sri Lanka's Hambantota port." *Financial Times* (December 11).

What OBOR is Not
(According to China)

After reading numerous items from various Chinese government English language sources on OBOR/BRI, one is left with a lingering question: "Does China protest too much?" Chinese commentaries on OBOR/BRI devote considerable space to tell their readers what the initiative is not.

In the January-February issue of *Foreign Affairs*, Mastro (2019) opened her article entitled "The Stealth Superpower: How China Hid It's Global Ambitions" with the following statement, 'China will not, repeat, not repeat the old practice of a strong country seeking hegemony,' Wang Yi, China's foreign minister, said last September. It was a message that Chinese officials have been pushing ever since their country's spectacular rise began."

Panda (2018) observed that:

China's Belt and Road Initiative (BRI) is creating ripples around the world because of its perceived hidden agenda of creating situations in which smaller nations engaging with BRI run the risk of falling into debt trap. China has spared no effort to portray its BRI, a grand trillion-dollar-plus global investment plan, as a positive vision for the world. But not everyone is convinced that it is such a great plan, either for China or for the countries it is investing in.

Most recently, a spokesman continued to defend his country's loan practices, as noted by Ghiglione (2019): "China takes the issue of debt seriously and within a project the Chinese side never imposes things nor, least of all, creates debt traps." Interestingly, the spokesman noted "Of course, like any international cooperation some problems and challenges may crop up. With experience it will improve."

The following phrases, taken collectively, are illustrative examples of what raises questions about China's stated intentions behind the OBOR/BRI. Many of these statements are taken from Wang Yiwei (2016), but similar comments have been take from other sources as well.

- The Belt and Road Initiative is **not** a plot.
- China is **not** attempting to rival US Naval Power in the global ocean.
- China will **not** seek maritime domination of the world.
- China will **not** "follow the old path of the Western powers which committed maritime expansion...."
- "The Belt and Road is by **no** means only one belt and one road."
- China's OBOR will **not** reconstruct the geo-political and the geo-economic world maps.
- China has **no** intention of overthrowing the existing international economic and financial system. A China renaissance "is **not** a threat to other countries."
- China is **not** isolationist.
- China is **not** just an agricultural society but an industrial society.
- China is **not** just a "Made in China" society but will be a "Built in China" society.
- China will **not** be just a participant in globalization but a "shaper" of it.
- OBOR is **not** a unilateral strategy for China's benefit.
- BRI is **not** an isolated one. It brings reform inside the country and links it to global free trade and well-being.
- BRI is **not** just a path option to realize the Chinese Dream, but also a strategic plan to enhance a rising power's voice."
- The OBOR/BRI is **not** like "The Marshall Plan." It excluded socialist countries and Third World countries. Therefore, it was the First World's assistance to the Second World.
- China is **not** a "free rider."
- China does **not** have geopolitical ambitions.
- China does **not** seek to create exclusionary blocs.
- China does **not** seek to impose business deals on others.
- The BRI does **not** aim at a geopolitical or military alliance.
- It will **not** establish a small bloc or set up a "China Club."
- China says projects **not** to blame for majority of Africa debt.

- China's involvement in Latin America has **nothing** to do with geopolitical competition.
- China's involvement in Latin America is nothing like a zero-sum game.
- Belt and Road is "never a geopolitical tool."
- China will not buckle in face of Belt and Road criticism.

Summing up these denials, China made the following assertions: China is not a hegemon trying to take control of the world's oceans. It has no hidden agenda other than to selflessly help other developing countries. It favors collective action over acting alone on the global stage. It is providing an alternative to current Western financial and political institutions. It favors globalization. That is the image that President Xi's China wants to convey to other countries.

REFERENCES

 Ghiglione, D., 2019. "Italy set to formally endorse China's Belt and Road Initiative." *Financial Times* (March 5).

 Mastro, O.S., 2019. "The Stealth Superpower: How China Hid Its Global Ambitions" *Foreign Affairs* (January-February).

 Panda, R., 2018. "China's BRI raises fears." *Deccan Herald* (September 23).

Wang, Yiwei., 2016. *The Belt and Road Initiative: What will China offer the world in its rise.* Reprinted 2018. (Beijing, China: New World Press). ISBN 978-7510455537.

OBOR (SWOC) Chart

Strengths, Weaknesses, Opportunities, and Constraints

The following SWOC assessment identifies OBOR's potential strengths, weaknesses, opportunities and constraints. It is illustrative, not comprehensive.

The United Nations Development Program (UNDP) came up with a way to quickly evaluate potential projects. It is a subjective approach, whether carried out alone or in a group, to identify the apparent strengths, weaknesses, opportunities and constraints, at least as a first approximation of the overall value to a government, society or community of the project being evaluated. The reason we note that the process is subjective is that perceptions of the value of a project can vary according to the perspective of the beholder. American singer Paul Simon once wrote that one person's ceiling may be another person's floor: what we consider a positive attribute of strength could be interpreted by another as an aspect of weakness. The weaknesses of a SWOC review notwithstanding, we considered it of some use to put together a SWOC chart as a brief glimpse of OBOR/BRI.

It is meant to be suggestive, illustrative and thought-provoking. It is neither definitive nor comprehensive. It is important to note that, depending on one's perceptions, a specific point could be placed in more than one category and that, for example, weaknesses and constraints could provide for opportunities for positive change and, therefore, strengths. An earlier SWOC list was compiled based on comments taken from various print and online sources for a short paper a couple of years ago. (Glantz, 2017) This has been updated to include comments up to early-2019.

Fig. 41 Is China strong enough to cope with the challenges generated by OBOR/BRI infrastructure objectives? *C. Stephens, SCMP*.

Strengths

- In theory, OBOR/BRI shares the prosperity of China with other developing countries.
- Provides Chinese expertise, knowledge and experience on transportation and trade infrastructure technology and construction.
- China's long-term perspective means likely long-term commitment.
- China's development model provides developing areas with a fast-track development model.
- In theory, China now promotes a green and low carbon infrastructure inside China, suggesting it is possible with its partners.
- OBOR/BRI avoids "hot" conflicts with other major powers, especially the US.
- It is an initiative to rebalance China's policy for Asia and to provide an alternative to dependence on US trade and aid.
- It keeps China's factories and factory workers employed.
- It expands markets abroad to absorb its industrial overcapacity.
- Developing countries have an alternative source (e.g., China-related development banks) for development funding to Western post-war financial institutions.
- China places fewer restrictions on loan arrangements with OBOR/BRI partners.

Weaknesses

- Economic and political instability in loan-recipient countries.
- Recipients have limited resources with which to repay their loan obligations.
- Loan contracts are done in secrecy by top government officials and have no transparency: Apparently there are non-disclosure clauses as in its SGR railroad agreement with Kenya.
- China's motives are mixed and unclear, and are constantly pointed out by those governments opposed to the Initiative, e.g., India and the US, among others.
- China has its own domestic economic vulnerabilities that are appearing in the current US-China trade war.
- Progress and success for any given infrastructure project are likely to be influenced by economic downturn (e.g., Chinese banks and companies are on a learning curve from their early experiences in OBOR/BRI, a trade war or a global recession).
- China and OBOR/BRI countries have religious and ethnic problems that are in conflict (as with China's crackdown on its Uighur population in western China's Xinjiang-Uighur Autonomous Region).
- Elections in loan-recipient countries can abruptly challenge the previous government's agreements (e.g., the corruption problem) and call for renegotiating the loans.
- China's "going green" as a high priority domestically, as called for now by President Xi, is at odds with the construction of coal-fired power plants and other adverse impacts on the environment of it OBOR/BRI projects.
- China professes to not take sides in domestic or regional political conflicts, which generates hostility and security threats toward the construction and eventual operation of its projects.
- Actions and statements from China are seen as aggressive toward others, regardless of reason: Its South China Sea nine-dash line; India's fear of China's Maritime Silk Road as an encircling "string of pearls;" Pakistan's CPEC with projects that run through the contested Pakistan-controlled parts of Kashmir.

Opportunities

- It provides the loan-recipient with desired and necessary domestic infrastructure to meet in-country and in-city transportation needs.
- It provides loan recipients' sorely-needed connectivity to regional and world trade hubs and markets.
- It provides access to China's markets for their exports.
- Opportunity to replicate the China development model by bypassing loan conditions of the World Bank and the IMF, for example.
- People-to-people participation can benefit citizens by providing educational opportunities in China.
- Opportunity for China to export the output of its overcapacity.
- Opportunity to send Chinese workers overseas.
- Opportunity to create or increase demand for China's products.
- Major European countries have shown interest in OBOR/BRI, despite US initial concerns (though they too have concerns of their own).
- Develops new opportunities for manufacturing, developing of industrial parks and creating hubs for distribution of goods and services.
- Further internationalization of China's currency, the RMB.
- China has been filling the geopolitical void in the international system in many areas, as a result of the US relinquishing it role as a world leader as it turns to isolationism.

Constraints (outside of China)

- Increasing concerns about loan conditions, e.g., Thailand, Malaysia and Indonesia have so far rejected some of the offers of support from China for infrastructure development.
- Conflict "hotspots" along the OBOR Eurasian land belt.
- Fear of China transferring its polluting industries to loan recipients.
- OBOR/BRI is seen by some as a proverbial "Trojan Horse" to a Chinese take over.
- Governments are beginning to question China's promises for development: "Not all that China touches is gold."
- Some loan recipients are concerned about the transferring of China's population to their OBOR/BRI partner countries, as Chinese workers choose not to return to China (e.g., as in the Philippines).
- China's response to security concerns for its infrastructure projects has led to a growth industry in China of security businesses or even the potential use of its troops to assure security for Chinese workers overseas.

Michael H. Glantz

- China's aggressive activities and intransigent political stance in the South China Sea.
- The dual use (civilian and military) of deep-water ports it has constructed is an apparent threat.
- A fear of falling into a debt trap has become a major concern, ever since China's 99-year takeover of the Sri Lankan port of Hambantota.
- Belated aggressive US moves to counter China's OBOR/BRI activities such as the "Made in China 2025" campaign.
- Negative perceptions about China's motives.
- Lingering concern about China's geopolitical ambitions.
- OBOR practices can conflict with local environmental protection and clean-up laws.
- Pressure on China to adopt other ways of doing business, such as opening up its markets, transparency, true multilateralism instead on secret bilateral agreements, and so forth.

REFERENCES

 Glantz M.H., 2017. "China's One Belt, One Road (Obor) Initiative: What A Difference A Brand Can Make." *Post-Soviet Issues*. 4(1): 8-19. (In Russian)

PART IV

Concluding Comments

Looking back to look ahead

The 2016 US election of President Trump, with his isolationist policies, sparked the US withdrawal from several American multilateral agreements, as well as an attack on globalization and on various United Nations agencies. This enabled President Xi's OBOR/BRI to establish the "Middle Kingdom" as the new major global political, economic power, and even as a military naval geopolitical force to be respected. Pitlo (2017) suggested that, "As things stand, with four more years of the Trump Administration, China will have the field wide open for its continued ascent into global power." This perception is reinforced by the many official "have no fear of China" pronouncements coming from Beijing about what OBOR/BRI is not.

China no longer accepts being fenced in by the United States and its allies on its eastern coast. By capturing the South China Sea, it has broken its virtual encirclement. Originally, OBOR was to connect China to Europe through Central Asia and the Middle East more efficiently and effectively; but it has since gone global. Linking its OBOR/BRI-related projects, or even just the deep-water ports it has built or updated, makes it clear that China is no longer a country whose interests are confined to Asia. Those making maps for OBOR's original six roads and belts have had difficulty keeping up with a graphic display of its strategic expansion. Most maps to date include neither Latin America nor the Arctic Maritime Silk Road as linked to OBOR/BRI.

The original interest in OBOR was sparked by OBOR as a brand. Lasting brands, however, survive "by consistently making good on what they promise to deliver." (Lewis, 2009) This will be a lesson Chinese authorities must keep in mind, if its OBOR/BRI Initiative is to be sustainable in the future.

China is on a path that can influence the world in a positive way through trade and infrastructure construction. Under the OBOR/BRI brand, Campbell (2017) has suggested, "China has wrapped an amorphous group of projects in a tidy package that speaks to inclusiveness, cooperation and altruism. It speaks of China: as an environmental leader, despite being the planet's worst polluter; as a champion of free trade and investment, despite wreathing its economy in protectionist red tape; as a good guy, despite acting as an authoritarian state that is a serial violator of human rights." Whether countries that have chosen to engage in such partnerships will be able to influence China's behavior through soft power remains to be seen.

Our overview of China's Belt and Road Initiative has raised the following ten observations of interest and concern.

(1) "Going Out" policy

A "going out" policy, raised by Chinese leaders in the late 1980s, turned into a global strategy in 2013 through the launching of the "One Belt One Road" (OBOR). The Initiative was the brainchild of Xi Jinping, newly elected to the presidency for a five-year term. However, within a few years, President Xi altered the Chinese constitution's limitation on the tenure of a president from only one term in office to no limits. President Xi was also able to add his signature OBOR economic initiative to the constitution. By going out regionally and globally through OBOR's "Silk Road" metaphor, President Xi attempted to provide Chinese-style development assistance to developing countries, whose leaders had watched China, the largest developing country, become a global economic power in just a few decades. The Chinese model of economic development provided hope through the possibility of Chinese loans for their desired national infrastructure projects.

(2) Geopolitical and invisible "Walls and Bridges"

There is some validity behind a perception captured in an article stating that "President Trump builds walls while China builds bridges." One example is that Trump immediately pulled the United States out of the Trans-Pacific Partnership (TPP) upon taking office in early 2017. China had opposed the TPP as an attempt by the United States to encroach on China's Asian neighbors. China lost no time in filling the political Pacific trade vacuum by strengthening trade agreements with its neighbors and increasing its activities in Pacific Rim countries such as those in Central and South America. Trump also began to challenge (attack, really) America's traditional defense agreements with its NATO allies (e.g., the UK, France, and Germany) as well as rewriting trade agreements with its closest neighbors, Mexico and Canada. Trump's increasingly restrictive immigration policies, not only with its southern neighbors, but also with potential immigrants from Muslim countries, asylum-seekers around the globe, foreign students, etc., suggest the building of an invisible political wall to block foreigners seeking to migrate to America.

The belief and expectation that China is building a sustainable bridge of friendship and a "partnership of equals" to developing countries through OBOR/BRI is increasingly being questioned by existing and potential development partners. China has had to take control of projects in countries where the governments proved unable to make their loan payments. As a result, questions again appeared about China's end game: becoming a global hegemon or being committed to humanitarian development assistance? It remains to be seen if China's bridge building is a political myth or a political reality.

(3) OBOR was a successful branding of a policy initiative

Without a doubt, the One Belt One Road Initiative (OBOR), later re-named the Belt and Road Initiative (BRI), has been a resounding success and a boon to Chinese leaders, banks and companies that supported "going out" regionally and globally. More than 70 countries and institutions have agreements with China through OBOR/BRI. Scores of developing country governments signed on to China's OBOR, because the Chinese government, banks and companies were offering loans to developing countries that would enable those countries to achieve their development hopes through sorely-needed infrastructure such as railways, highways, pipelines, deep-water ports, and even airports. Under the guise of multilateralism, China often engaged in loan negotiations bilaterally and in secrecy (i.e., with a lack of transparency), without having to invoke usual loan concerns of Western development banks such as high interest rates, the borrowers'

ability to repay their loans, political stability, their human rights record, over-looking sovereignty conflicts, or levels of corruption.

(4) Is the BRI re-brand unraveling at the 5-year OBOR anniversary mark?

At the five-year anniversary mark for the OBOR/BRI Initiative, there is increasing concern that China's OBOR/BRI developing country partners are in a debt trap with China as the beneficiary. While there is no reason to believe that was the goal of China's initiative, it was a possibility, and now it has happened to some OBOR partners such as Sri Lanka, Tajikistan, and most recently in Zambia. India has warned about the debt trap for some time. There have been second thoughts by some countries in their negotiations with China for OBOR/BRI infrastructure projects (Malaysia, Myanmar, Sierra Leone, Pakistan, etc.).

(5) China's "Great Games"

The notion of "Great Games" is really about a geopolitical competition for "spheres of influence" among regional and global powers. It is much broader than the original competitive situation between two empires, the Russian and the British, in Central Asia in the late 1800s. One way to look at the Great Games in Asia, Latin America, and Africa, is that they can be discussed as a competition among countries to secure political and economic (e.g., functional) spheres of influence. Spheres can be based on territorial propinquity, as suggested by China's neighborhood policy. The competition in Central Asia can involve China, Russia and India; in South Asia – Russia, China, Iran, Saudi Arabia, India, and Pakistan; in Latin America – China and the United States competing for potential influence in the Western Hemisphere. Spheres of influence and the notion of Great Games also apply to situations where there is competition for functional dominance between countries over activities such as global digital communications and the use of space.

(6) How significant are China's comments about "What OBOR/BRI is not"?

Reading scores of articles about China's OBOR/BRI activities, it might be easy to overlook how every so often there is an official statement about what President Xi's infrastructure development assistance is not. After a

Michael H. Glantz

while, you come to realize that there are many such statements made by officials, writers, and in the electronic media. Even President Xi has referred to what OBOR was not designed to be or do; for example, OBOR is not about China becoming a global hegemon, or about China seeking client states through loan defaults by OBOR partners (e.g., purposely setting up debt traps). Taken collectively, one might wonder whether China was protesting too much in order to make clear what OBOR/BRI was not!

(7) The Silk Road image is a traditional Chinese political slogan

The silk road and the maritime belt are similar in function to Chinese political campaigns and sloganeering, for which the Maoist period of China was so famous. The political campaigns were primarily for domestic consumption and slogans were designed to encourage (if not force) Chinese citizens to help the Communist Party energize the populace to achieve its political objectives. Silk road activities are for foreign as well as for domestic objectives. The foreign objectives were to energize and encourage developing countries to borrow from Chinese institutions in order to meet their infrastructure needs more easily and more quickly for economic development purposes as well as to spread China's influence. The domestic aspect of the silk roads initiative involved energizing Chinese corporations to go abroad with their products and workers to keep their manufacturing processes working at full steam and send Chinese workers abroad to work on OBOR/BRI infrastructure projects.

(8) How significant is China's use of the word "One"?

The word "One" is more than just a number. It can have several meanings. For the Beijing Olympics theme in 2008 the "One" in "One World One Dream" was used to inspire a competitive spirit and the feeling of oneness, solidarity, of world athletes. It apparently was expected that the same word "one" could serve as a symbol for unity and equality among China's international development partners in its One Belt One Road Initiative. However, to potential recipients of China's infrastructure loans, its use in the OBOR context apparently left open the possibility that China would remain in the driver's seat in any project partnerships that might develop. The official acronym was changed to BRI, Belt and Road Initiative. Shepard (2017b) observed that "while OBOR is no longer the name of the initiative, it is still the same top-down

plan to build new ports, roads, railways, power plants and special economic zones across Asia and Africa to integrate the entire region into a massive market spanning 60 countries and a third of the world's GDP [Gross Domestic Product]." Shepard went on to note that a Google comparison of the use of the OBOR and BRI acronyms showed "OBOR and One Belt One Road are still more commonly used than Belt and Road."

Today, China professes to be interested in multilateral activities. However, it tends to remains apart from countries (e.g., the Group of 77+1 of Non-aligned Nations or, more recently, the Group of 16+1 in Central, Eastern and Southeastern Europe). China, similarly to other countries, puts its sovereignty above collective action, though it is a member of multilateral organizations. China has veto power in the UN and also disregards decisions that it views to be against its national interests, e.g., the International Court of Justice decision against China's takeover of islands in the South China Sea.

While China may have become somewhat more open to multilateralism, one paper noted that "Chinese understanding of multilateralism is very much different from the European one." The same paper did acknowledge that "Traditionally, the preference of Chinese policy was bilateralism or even unilateralism. From the 1990s, especially in the 21st Century, China paid more attention to multilateralism." (Song, 2010) However, OBOR/BRI projects are basically bilateral endeavors, with less transparency.

(9) OBOR/BRI is changing politically, economically, militarily

Ever since the launching of OBOR, change has been one of its constant characteristics. New partnerships between China and countries emerged monthly during the past five years along the various silk roads and the maritime belts. Latin American countries, still not shown by China on its official OBOR maps, have become OBOR/BRI-like partners to China. Neglected by the United States for the past couple of decades, Latin countries are eager for funds to develop their economies, and modern infrastructure is considered a necessary condition for economic development.

The geopolitical aspects of China's OBOR/BRI have become increasingly apparent. It has now set itself on a course to challenge the dominance of the West in economics as well as in politics. Project partnerships with China based on its loans for infrastructure can lead to special influence on their recipients' internal political situations. In other words, partners can become client states or, as some observers have suggested, they are candidates to become China's colonies.

OBOR/BRI also has a growing military dimension. As a result of a more aggressive stance toward taking ownership of islands and atolls in the South China Sea, China has built up the islands and developed them as military bases. In their OBOR/BRI partnership with Djibouti, China has developed a military base that could house 10,000 troops. It is China's first overseas base and is the result of China's development of a deep-water port there. In addition, Djibouti is a terminal point for a high-speed rail line from Ethiopia's capital, Addis Ababa. This presence at a strategic place on the Indian Ocean is a major concern in India about its encirclement by Chinese deep-water infrastructure projects. A third example of military outreach would be the Chinese Space Station and space antenna in Argentina's Patagonia Desert, a station that can monitor communications in the Western Hemisphere and has implications for the militarization of space.

The latest changes under the BRI acronym relate to challenges and changes brought about by China's partners. They are raising concerns about their OBOR/BRI loans for infrastructure as debt traps. China makes the loans and when the recipient countries cannot meet their loan obligations the Chinese take over ownership and/or control of the project. Some countries have reduced the size of their loans by reducing the size of their infrastructure schemes to manageable levels.

(10) Do Regional Organizations have an Achilles Heel?

Each regional organization, whose core members are sovereign countries, has as its stated goal, unity. They come together for a host of reasons mainly to have a stronger voice in regional as well as global affairs. Besides, countries in a given region likely share or face similar political, economic and societal problems. Countries also join together for ideological reasons. They join together because of perceived outsiders' threats, (e.g., "United we stand. Divided we fall."); or by common positive interests (e.g., "there is strength in numbers"). In any event, unity is a *raison d'être* to join together, but a country's commitment to regional unity is not necessarily its highest priority. Member states are not equal in size however, differing in economic stability, political influence and military power. Some members are more in need of development assistance than are others.

Each region and sub-region in Southeast Asia, Africa, Greater Europe and Latin America, has its own political organization to address regional issues: ASEAN, Africa Union (AU), the European Union (EU), and the Organization of America States (OAS), respectively. Reviewing China's OBOR/BRI-related activities in each of these regions, China has made inroads, through infrastructure and trade-related loans to one or more states that have the potential to weaken that drive for unity. As noted earlier, documented debt traps have already happened with Greece and Hungary resulting in the taking of lone positions that differed from the EU on China's human rights record and other current actions. Debt traps have also happened in South and Central America because of factors that are either push (US inattention) or pull (loans from China). China sees Southeast Asia as in its SOI and has made separate negotiations with various members of ASEAN concerning its take-over of reefs and islands in the South China Sea. The adage "divide and conquer" comes to mind. Each regional organization has, in other words, its proverbial Achilles heel, when it comes to dealing with China's OBOR/BRI.

REFERENCES

 Campbell, C., 2017. "Ports, Pipelines and Geopolitics: China's New Silk Road is a Challenge for Washington." *TIME* (October 23).

 Lewis, K., 2009. "How to Maintain A Brand." *Forbes* (May 15).

 Pitlo III, L.B., 2017. "As America's Image Falters, China's Confidence Grows." *China-US Focus* (June 22).

 Shepard, W., 2017b. "Beijing to the World: Don't Call the Belt and Road Initiative OBOR." *Forbes* (August 1).

 Song, X., 2010. "China and Regional Integration: From Bilateralism to Regional-Multilateralism." *The IUP Journal of International Relations.* SSRN (April 22).

Michael H. Glantz

Glimpsing the Future: Thucydides's Trap

American Political Scientist and Harvard University professor Graham Allison identified a concept called "Thucydides's trap" in an article published in the *Financial Times* entitled "Thucydides's trap has been sprung in the Pacific." Five years later Allison (2017) expanded the idea in his book, *Destined for War: Can America and China Escape Thucydides's Trap?*

Two thousand four hundred years ago, Athenian citizen Thucydides wrote about the Peloponnesian Wars between Athens (a rising power) and Sparta (the established power at the time). Allison (2012) noted that Thucydides had written "It was the rise of Athens and the fear that this inspired in Sparta that made war inevitable." Allison continued: "Classical Athens was at the center of civilization.... [Its] dramatic rise shocked Sparta.... Fear compelled its leaders to respond. Threat and counter-threat produced competition, then confrontation and finally conflict. At the end of 30 years of war, both states had been destroyed."

Allison (2017) studied 17 conflict situations, 12 of which he labeled as a "Thucydides's trap." In his article (Allison, 2012) he noted: "The defining question about global order in the decades ahead will be: can China and the US escape the Thucydides's trap? The historian's metaphor reminds us of the dangers two parties face when a rising power rivals a ruling power – as Athens did in the 5th century BC and Germany did at the end of the 19th century. Most such challenges have ended in war." The idea of such a trap has generated considerable discussion about the current relationship between President Xi Jinping and President Donald Trump.

The US became the leader of the non-Communist

Fig. 42 Thucydides' history reveals the dangers of extended conflict. *SCRIBE Publications.*

world at the end of World War II, fostering alliances around the globe to contain the Soviet Union and China, and their expansion of Communist ideology and territorial take-over. The Soviet Union began to dissolve in the late 1980s. At that time, China began a decades-long process toward emerging as a global economic power. Under President Xi Jinping's rule in 2013 and the launching of his flagship "One Belt One Road Initiative" program, China's goal to regain past glory as a political and military power has put it on a competitive path with the United States for what it sees as its rightful place as a global superpower.

In an editorial entitled "Are we at America's 'peak'?", Zacharia (2018) commented on worrisome changes in US behavior in international affairs as well as in China's behavior. He suggested that such changes are leading to a potentially dangerous situation between these two global powers, the former power on the decline and the latter power on the rise. Zacharia stated his observation succinctly in the following way:

The smart path to constraining China comes not from a head-on policy of containment but rather from a subtle one that forces Beijing to remain enmeshed and interdependent with the international community. China recognizes this and tries hard to free itself from multilateral groups, preferring to deal one-on-one with countries where it will always tower over its negotiating partner. And yet, nothing animates the Trump administration more than its opposition to multilateralism of any kind. And so the world gets more chaotic.

China has been building up its economic and political presence on all continents through Xi's OBOR Initiative (officially, Belt and Road Initiative). OBOR presents an alternative for risky (corrupt, poor or unstable) countries to meet their infrastructure-related development needs, by providing loans that Western governments and their institutions would refuse to make without strict requirements, including transparency, on the use of those funds. China also makes clear to the prospective borrower that it is not concerned about a loan-seeking country's internal political issues or conflicts. Its OBOR-related *modus operandi* is in clear contrast with those of the World Bank and the IMF. An important key factor is that China has had the "cash" to undertake such projects. China apparently wins, at least in the short term, regardless of the viability of the loans, because it has taken control of some assets when loans could not be recovered.

The international and domestic policies of the United States during the time of President Trump have made China's rise to global power status extremely easy, as a result of Trump's nationalistic, isolationist, "America First" policies, including (but not limited to): building a wall along its border with Mexico to block migration from Mexico and Central America; attacks on its alliances such as NATO and NAFTA; withdrawal from international agreements on climate change and on Iran. Trump has challenged China's trade and other commercial practices and initiated a trade war with China (and also with US allies as well) by tacking high tariffs on to basic imports. China, of course, has retaliated. The trade war escalates.

Holmes (2018) succinctly captured the following perception about Xi's China and Trump's United States:

It was the best of times, it was the worst of times. A tale of two world leaders, U.S. president Donald Trump and China president Xi Jinping – both of whose countries have among the world's best economies right now. But whereas Xi is playing Santa Claus to the rest of the world, doling out loans to finance-starved countries, Trump is playing Scrooge, waging an economic war with Canada, the European Union, China and others.

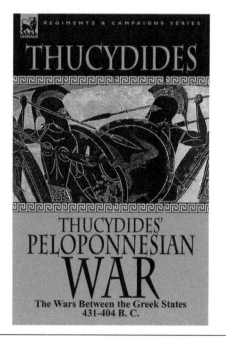

Can we avoid the 'Thucydides Trap'?
-The Japan Times

The Thucydides Trap: How to stop the looming war between China and the U.S.
-The Big Think

US-China trade war: toward the Thucydides Trap?
-Washington Post

There Is No Thucydides Trap
-SupChina

The Thucydides Trap: Are the U.S. and China Headed for War?
-Belfer Center

Is the world spiraling down towards Thucydides Trap?
-South Morning China Post

How Trump and China's Xi could stumble into war
- The Washington Post

Thucydides Trap: Destined for War
-Harvard Kennedy School

How to Avoid the Thucydides Trap: The Missing Piece
-The Diplomat

Can America and China Avoid the Pull of the Thucydides Trap?
-The National Interest

Fig. 43 Recent media headlines referring to the Thucydides's Trap in relation to the current US-China trade war of 2018-19 and foreign policy. *The Peloponnesian Wars* was written by Thucydides 2400 year ago. *Houghton Mifflin Harcourt.*

Michael H. Glantz

To China, Trump's US appears politically and economically weak, burdened with a large and growing foreign debt, and bogged down by wars in Southwestern Asia. Trump is also distracted by investigations into election-related problems. To the US, Xi's China is faced with increasing domestic opposition about his economy and about his authoritarian decision-making processes that consolidate his control over party and country. An increasing number of opinions appearing in the media are about America's decline as a superpower and about China's rise as a superpower. There has also been considerable discussion around the validity of the Thucydides's trap, as suggested in the headlines in the preceding graphic.

Which country is likely to dominate the 21st century?

An activity that political pundits tend to engage in, at the end of one century and the beginning of the next, is to ponder the following questions: "whose century was it?" or "whose century will the next one be?" These questions invoke highly biased answers. As examples, one could argue that the 1500s were dominated by Portugal because of its exploration in Africa and Asia; the 1600s belong to Dutch mercantilism; the 1700s to the French, in large measure because of the French Revolution; the 1800s by the British Empire because of its colonies and its control of the seas. The 1900s illustrate how difficult it is to make such a determination: the American century? The Soviet Union's century? the European century?

Today, there are two popular choices when it comes to suggesting which country might dominate the 21st Century: the United States and China. Speculation abounds, as suggested by the following headlines:

- "China's Eurasian Century?";
- "Will the 21st century 'belong' to China?";
- "The 21st Century Another American Century? Don't Bet on It.";
- "US vs. China: Whose century is it, anyway."
- "If the 20th century was America's, is the 21st China's?"

As stated today, China's OBOR/BRI is an aspirational goal to be reached by mid-century. Mid-century, 2049 to be exact, is the official time that the initiative is to be completed as it will be the 100th anniversary of the Mao's Chinese Communist Party victory in 1949.

China's Communist Party and Government have operational goals along the way to achieving geopolitical superpower status. It appears, from the perspective of 2019, that the aspirational road to achieve its mid-century goal is still possible and likely by 2049, if not earlier. As has been said about "all roads leading to Rome," there are now many roads to Beijing and a successful OBOR/BRI. Which road(s) China will ultimately take will depend on what its leaders want to see and do along the way. The strategy for mid-century remains fixed in stone – to become a global superpower to be reckoned with – but the shorter term operational (tactical) goals can change day by day, month by month, or year by year, depending on obstacles encountered while realizing its aspirational goal in a few decades from now. However, some authors have already made their decision: "In the 19th century, the world was Europeanized. In the 20th century, it was Americanized. Now, in the 21st century, the world is being Asianized." (Khanna, 2019)

Fig. 44 This political cartoon suggests China's "Game Plan" for superpower status by 2049. *C. Stephens, SCMP.*

REFERENCES

Allison, G., 2017. *Destined for War: Can America and China Escape Thucydides's Trap?* Boston, MA: Houghton Mifflin Harcourt. ISBN 978-0544935273.

 Allison, G., 2012. "Graham Allison on U.S.-China relations." *Belfer Center in the News* (August 22).

 Holmes, F., 2018. "China's Belt and Road Initiative Opens Up Unprecedented Opportunities." *U.S. Global Investors* (September 4).

Khanna, P., 2019. *The Future is Asian*. Simon & Schuster. ISBN 978-1501196263.

 Zacharia, F., 2018. "Are we at 'peak America'?" *The Washington Post* (November29).

Appendices

Image Sources

Fig. 1   Consortium for Capacity Building (CCB).

Fig. 2   Turpan street artist.

Fig. 3   C. Stephens. https://www.scmp.com/comment/insight-opinion/article/1399681/chinas-overcapacity-crisis-can-spur-growth-through-overseas

Fig. 4   Dave Simmonds. https://www.economist.com/china/2016/07/02/our-bulldozers-our-rules

Fig. 5   B. Krajnik. http://www.sloveniatimes.com/belt-and-road-for-international-cooperation

Fig. 6   Wikipedia.

Fig. 7   A. van Dam.

Fig. 8   Xiao Yong. http://olympic-museum.de/pmedals/olympic-games-participation-medals-2008.php

Fig. 9   Cheah Sinann. https://www.toonpool.com/cartoons/One%20Belt%20One%20Road_293876

Fig. 10   Lommes. Wikipedia. https://commons.wikimedia.org/w/index.php?curid=58884083

Fig. 11   CCB.

Fig. 12   Headlines from various media. CCB.

Fig. 13   U.S. Chamber of Commerce.

Fig. 14   CCB. Adapted from Julianna Wu.

Fig. 15   D. Reljic, BOLD. https://www.boldbusiness.com/infrastructure/chinas-1-trillion-dollar-world-project/

Fig. 16   CCB. Adapted from Xia Qing/GT.

Fig. 17   Tupian 114, China Dream.

Fig. 18   Woodrow Wilson Center Press.

Fig. 19   Youtube, Global Conflict. https://www.youtube.com/watch?v=d0QS9Be0K-0

Fig. 20   Youtube, Pakistan Observer. https://pakobserver.net/cpec-corridor-opportunities/

Fig. 21   Chad Crowe. https://blogs.timesofindia.indiatimes.com/all-that-is-solid-melts/cpec-is-a-sea-change-it-transforms-the-matrix-of-opportunities-and-threats-in-indias-neighbourhood/

Fig. 22   David Parkins. https://www.researchgate.net/publication/318742639_Dragon_and_Bear_A_SF-MDA_Approach_to_Intersemiotic_Relations

Fig. 23   Gautier de Blonde. forums.airbase.ru/2012/06/t34782_21--nauchno-issledovatelskie-suda.html

Fig. 24   CCB.

Fig. 25   CCB.

FIG. 26   A. Rae. http://aseansection.blogspot.com/2014/04/

FIG. 27   CCB.

FIG. 28   Peter Shrank. https://www.economist.com/leaders/2016/11/17/try-persist-persevere

Fig. 29   Schiller Institute. http://newparadigm.schillerinstitute.com/blog/2018/01/21/u-s-must-join-chinas-belt-road-developing-caribbean-central-america/

Fig. 30   CCB.

Fig. 31   CCB.

Fig. 32   CEE Institute.

Fig. 33   CCB.

Fig. 34   Skilla 1st. https://commons.wikimedia.org/wiki/File:Map_of_Addis_Ababa-Djibouti_Railway.png

Fig. 35   Victor Ndula. https://www.pulse.com.gh/communities/bloggers/the-china-africa-project-is-china-colonizing-africa-id5062989.html

Fig. 36   P.E.O. Usher.

Fig. 37   NOAA. https://celebrating200years.noaa.gov/transformations/gps/Figure_1.html

Fig. 38   M.H. Glantz, CCB.

Fig. 39   Care2 Petition.

Fig. 40   CCB, adapted from Anon.

Fig. 41   C. Stephens. https://www.scmp.com/comment/insight-opinion/article/2085812/why-china-isnt-ready-be-global-leader

Fig. 42   SCRIBE Publications.

Fig. 43   Headlines from various media. Book cover, Houghton Mifflin Harcourt.

Fig. 44   C. Stephens, South China Morning Post.

About the Authors

Michael H. Glantz was a Senior Scientist at the National Center for Atmospheric Research (NCAR), where he researched from 1974 to 2009. Since then, he has been the director of the University of Colorado's Consortium for Capacity Building (CCB). His research publications relate to understanding how extreme climate, water and weather affect societies and how societies affect climate. Since 1976, Glantz has conducted joint research in the former Soviet Union and in the Central Asian Republics on desertification and on the disappearing of the Aral Sea. In 2013 he was recognized by China as a pioneer in desertification studies. Glantz is a member of the Advisory Committee of the international Integrated Risk Governance Program, headquartered at Beijing Normal University. He has lectured on the Climate Affairs concept in several Chinese cities at universities and meteorological centers. He has numerous publications on climate, water and weather issues. Glantz and Professor Qian (BNU and executive director of the IRG) co-authored *Usable Thoughts*: *Climate, Water and Weather in the 21st Century*. His current multiyear research is "El Niño Ready Nations," supported by USAID/OFDA. Many Belt and Road countries are affected by El Niño's impacts.

In 1990 he received the Global 500 Award of the UN Environment Program (UNEP) that recognizes people working in diverse ways to protect and enhance the planet's natural resources.

Glantz received the 2009 Clinton Global Initiative and Rockefeller Foundation Commitment.

He has a BS in Metallurgical Engineering (1961) and an MA (1963) and PhD (1970) in Political Science/ International Relations from the University of Pennsylvania.

Robert J. Ross is Project Manager and Research Assistant for CCB. He has been researching societal and environmental issues that result from climate variability, change and extremes. He was invited to attend Beijing Normal University's summer program for Disaster Risk Reduction (DRR) in 2015, which was focused on social responsibility in Early Warning Systems. He is currently researching an approach to earlier warnings of societal risks of El Niño's global impacts.

Gavin Goldstein Daugherty earned an MSc degree in Global Politics, Conflict Studies, at the London School of Economics and Political Science (LSE). His research focused on macroeconomic and political analyses of the China-South China Sea and the Russia-Crimea disputes. Prior to attending LSE, Daugherty earned a BA in Political Science from the University of Colorado – Boulder, where he also worked as a Research Assistant at the Consortium for Capacity Building. Daugherty's research interests include international relations and their economic impacts in the Eurasian region.

CPSIA information can be obtained
at www.ICGtesting.com
Printed in the USA
LVHW071611230120
644586LV00022B/1771